Preface

THIS book is a manifesto on the concept of human beings keeping other human beings in cages, and the effects of that on both society and the individual. The story is composed of a number of events that I experienced directly, and they are one-hundred percent true. The structure of my composition is intentional, and it is intended to convey my actual state of mind at the time of the events depicted. There are several passages where I refer to myself in the third person. This was both how I felt about myself at times, and it was necessary while writing and re-writing in order to keep going. There are also vignettes that involve some of my more pronounced memories during childhood. These helped me make it through my ordeal at the supermax.

The process of writing is a lot like the process of personal growth and development. I began this work with an idea, sketched out the general framework and then began to put the meat on the bones. Of course, I had to go over the whole thing time and time again in order to get it the way I wanted it to be. The act of writing has been my main therapy for many years now. I may or may not be a good writer (that is for you to decide), but I love to write. A lot of what you are about to read was first written with the stub of a pencil on lined, prison-supplied paper. There is a lot of written content that has been lost to transfers, shakedowns, and broken sprinklers. It does not bother me because it was always the process itself that was most important to me. There are more stories within the story that could have been told. However, I decided to keep it as short and to-the-point as is possible in order to sharpen the points I want to make. Perhaps I will revisit the rest of the story at another time. For now, it is more than sufficient for the purposes it is intended to fulfill. I am confident that the reader will find this work to be educational, practical, and useful particularly for those who are interested in criminal justice system reform. My main point is that there are better ways to achieve the goals of law and order in our society. Thought I do carry a certain hurt in my heart, I am not bitter or vindictive or unfair.

D1707459

0

The Supermax Prison

THE bus slows and makes a heavy turn into the Federal Correctional Complex in Florence, Colorado. It pauses at the guard station near the entrance before lumbering up a grade. On the left are what look like college dormitories or condominiums but is the low security camp. To the right, the Federal Correctional Institution commonly called an F.C.I. appears. It has fences around it but no guard towers. This is a medium security prison, and it is larger than the camp. The bus downshifts and shakes a bit as it continues uphill and around the curves. The prisoners look to the left where the United States Penitentiary sprawls out below the roadway. This is a maximum-security institution that has a lot of razor wire, guard towers, and perimeter patrol trucks. But the bus keeps going up the hill, veers slightly to the right, and stops beside a giant guard tower made of concrete. Some of the prisoners move around in their seats. The bus has arrived at the Administrative Maximum Facility, the "Supermax."

The guards take turns divesting themselves of their weapons and ammunition, and it seems there are a lot of them. The outer gate slides open and the bus crawls into a sally port area and shudders to a silence. The outer gate closes. The guards begin a methodical search of the bus. They open all of the storage hatches on the outside of the bus and look underneath it with mirrors affixed to long poles. They make a cursory look into every compartment and enter the bus to count the prisoners. The buildings are low to the ground and nondescript: prefabricated concrete with a faux brick laminate on the outer walls, and no windows. The outer fences have a lot of razor wire between them and are obviously electrified. The perimeter patrols zip around in white pickup trucks. The inner gate finally opens, the bus driver hops in and starts the engine, releases the air brakes, and eases through. There are numerous guards who walk beside the bus as it moves around the right side of the building at a snail's pace....

Down the side of the building a ways, the pavement ends at what looks like a big garage door. It opens slowly and the bus has to wait for the pneumatic security barriers to recede into the concrete before it can pull into the inside of the building. It is like a big garage with nothing in it, and the lighting is low. The bus pulls straight ahead and noses up to a spot where a boxcar-type steel door is in close proximity. The prisoners are silent. There is a palpable tension in the air. There is another period of time spent in waiting before the boxcar door opens and a number of prison staff appear. They line up by the door of the bus, one holding a video camera. A burly lieutenant enters the bus and yells, "Powers, John!"

1

*Everyone is looking around to see who is getting off. I am slow
to stand because of the chains and the fact that I cannot use my
hands and arms. I shuffle for the ward down the aisle. There
are prisoners on both sides, and they are looking at me. I stop
near the gate at the front of the bus. The Lieutenant tells me to
recite my prisoner registration number, and I do that. Then I
turn and face the other prisoners and tell them I wish them all
good luck and to keep their spirits up. Some of them reply in
kind. The Lieutenant keys the gate and stares at me as I pass
him and proceed down the steps. I am suddenly surrounded by
the staff and walked inside the Receiving and Discharged
(R&D) area of the facility. I am immediately placed in a
holding cell to the right, and the guards remove the lock, belly
chain, and the black box while I face the wall. They instruct me
to remain there while they back out of the holding cell. They
then remove the shackles, hand cuffs through the bars and tell
me to strip off all the clothing and putt everything through the
bars. I comply and soon find myself standing naked in front of
strangers – one of whom is holding a video camera on me.*

GUARD: All right, open your mouth. Wider, Lift your upper lip. Now the
lower… any dentures, braces or other things in your mouth?

POWERS: Nope.

GUARD: Fingers through your hair. Bend forward so I can see. All right.
Let me see behind your right ear. Now the left Hands out like this. Wiggle
your fingers. Turn your hands over, palms up. Okay. Raise your arms over
your head. Now, lift your dick. Lift your dick and balls. All right. Turn
around, bend over and spread your cheeks. Bottom of your left foot wiggle
the toes. And the right foot. Okay, now squat and cough.

POWERS: That doesn't work, you know.

GUARD: What's that?

POWERS: The old "squat and cough" thing. It doesn't work. You think if
you have something inside your rectum and you squat and cough, it is going
to fall out?

GUARD: It's policy. All you need to do is whatever I tell you to do.

POWERS: Well, try it when you get home today. Stick something up your ass and then squat and cough and see if it comes out. I bet it won't.

This exchange pisses them off and makes them suspect I am hiding something in my ass. They have a conference with the lieutenant at the desk, and he makes some phone calls. I am not trying to be a smartass. I am pointing out that this "procedure" has no legitimate value in terms of security. I do not realize that the procedure is not really about security; it is about control. They want me to know that they are the ones who are calling the shots and that they can do pretty much anything they want to whether it makes sense or not.

They have me dress in boxers, elastic waisted pants, and a pull over shirt, all tan in color. Then I am provided with a pair of white socks and a pair of blue "boat shoes" that I slip on. They handcuff me through the bars and put a square contraption called a Black Box over the chain between the handcuffs. This device covers the keyholes and makes it impossible to move your hands in any direction. They tell me to turn around, and they apply the shackles to my ankles and double lock them. They make sure everyone is ready before unlocking the gate and telling me to back out. They grab me and put my face to the wall while they put what is called a Martin chain around my waist. It connects to the Black Box and is secured with a heavy padlock.

They proceed to take fingerprints, photographs and swabs for their DNA database. It is like being booked in at a county jail. They stand all around with clubs in their hands, waiting for me to try them--like I could do anything at all with fifty pounds of chains and locks on me... They parade me through a set of electronically controlled solid steel doors, down a short corridor with mounted cameras at each end, and into the medical department. There is a big modern x-ray machine in the middle of the floor. Some weird dude with glasses and a lab coat makes sure I am positioned in the way he wants, and then begins taking x-rays of me chains and all. He takes so many x-rays I begin to feel like one of the test chimpanzees in the movie Project X.

Finally, I am escorted out of the R&D area and down a long hallway. No one is talking. It is only the sound of keys jangling and squashy footsteps. There are two or three guards behind me, one who still has a video camera on me and a couple on each side of me, including the Lieutenant. The clubs they are carrying are about 3-feet long and have what looks like stainless steel balls imbedded at the tip.

They do not carry them carelessly, either; they have them ready to strike. Their radios crackle every once in a while as we make our way along the wide but asymmetrical corridors. I cannot walk too well due to the metal cutting into my ankles and the short chain between the shackles. I am shuffling along at a snail's pace.

We seem to be going deeper into the bowels of the building. We go through more barred gates, down a slope, turn sharply to the right, and then go down a steep slope. I am numb in my mind and fatigued in my body. We come to a halt in front of a green boxcar door with the words "Control Unit" stenciled over it. The lieutenant speaks into his radio, and, after a moment, the door slides open and clacks. We step inside a sally port area and the outer door slides closed with another clack. We wait again, and then the sally port door slides open, and we proceed down a short and narrow hallway inside the unit.

Up ahead is an enclosed module they call the control bubble. There is a guard inside it, monitoring cameras and opening and closing doors from a panel of switches and lights. There are narrow gates on each side of the bubble; the one on the right opens as we get there, and we walk on through. We bear to the right and go up a short flight of steps, through yet another gate, and onto the upper range. The cells are on the righthand side of the range. On the left-hand side are indoor recreation areas that have nothing in them except a chin-up bar. There are big windows made of safety glass all the way down through the indoor recreation areas and, of course surveillance cameras.

About three quarters of the way down the range one of the cell doors opens. We pass cells on the right, and I see prisoners in some of them, but some of them are darkened as well. The cells are all side-by-side in a row that goes straight to the end of the range. There are thirteen cells all together. The cell fronts have a solid steel boxcar door with a food hatch built in and a fairly good-sized window made of the same thick safety glass and backed by oversized vertical bars on the inside. My entourage pauses to direct me into cell number 208. There is a sally port just past the outer door. They tell me to turn around and to walk backwards into the cell area when the sally port door opens.

The guard with the video camera steps inside the sally port and keeps filming. Another guard begins to remove all of the locks and chains in what must be some kind of a security sequence. He removes the Black Box and handcuffs last. They then back out of the sally port one by one, and the cameraman finally finishes the filming of my arrival. The outer door closes, and the locking mechanisms clank into place. Powers has arrived at the Alcatraz of the Rockies as Federal Bureau of Prisons staff refer to it the impenetrable supermax.

It is the day after Christmas and there is a lot of snow on the ground outside. My older brother and I both received new bicycles. We are excited to have them, but we cannot ride them because of the snow. I am not thinking too much about it and get wrapped up doing other things. But when I go to find my brother, I see he is outside and has cleared a space in the front yard and has my new bicycle turned upside down and has removed the wheels and is in the process of switching the wheels on his bike for mine. I run to tell Mom and she goes out on the porch to yell at him. He does not stop, though he evens ends up switching seats because he likes the one I got better than the one he got.

Inside Cell 208

THERE is hair all over the cell like the prior resident pulled his hair out in clumps. There is nothing else in the cell except for a beat-up old mattress on a raised slab of concrete they call a bunk. Powers goes to the narrow vertical window at the back of the cell and sees a brick wall a few feet away. He angles his head and stoops down enough to see a sliver of blue sky over the top of the brick wall. He thinks, maybe this place is underground after all. There is a spider in a dusty web in the corner. Powers touches the web and the spider scrambles only to find it has been a false alarm.

There is a shower inside the cell. It is made from sheets of stainless steel that are welded together to form an elongated box. There is a button on the inside that, when pushed, runs the shower for about a minute before needing to be pushed again. There is a lot of hair in the shower; it is collected around the drain in a circular design that looks something like a bird's nest. "They need to give me some cleaning supplies," Powers says out loud. He presses the button that is called a duress button and the guard from the bubble immediately comes on the intercom mounted in the sally port:

GUARD: What is your medical emergency?

POWERS: I need to get some cleaning supplies. This cell is a filthy mess.

GUARD: The duress button is to be used for medical emergencies only. If you press it again, I will write an incident report.

POWERS: Go right ahead and start writing. This cell is nasty, and I need something to clean it wit and I need my regular issue. I have nothing: no linen, no clean clothing, no towels or washcloths, no soap, shampoo nothing!

GUARD: You will get what you have coming, nothing more and nothing less. You do need to calm down, though. You just got here and already you are causing a disturbance.

POWERS: What? A disturbance? You call this a disturbance? I have been on a bus since three-thirty this morning. I need food and water and a shower, and I need to lie down! You people could have at least made sure this cell was cleaned. Now you are making me wait for what should have already been issued. It's bullshit!

GUARD: You'd better get used to it, Powers. You are going to be here for a long time, and you are better off to go with the program and not cause trouble.

POWERS: Or what? You'll put me in the ADX?

It is all boxes. The concept of crime and punishment in America is all about putting people into boxes and making sure they stay put. This is a box within a box within a box. The air is stale, the paint is pale gray and pea green and off white. It is a steel and concrete sarcophagus. I have been buried alive, and this I no bullshit. It is not much different than being kidnapped and placed in some kind of a box the ground. They feed you, give you water, toilet facilities and ventilation. It would be much more humane if they had simply put a bullet into the back of my head and been done with it. This kind of thing is insidious far more insidious than anything I have ever done. No one can ever convince me that I did anything even close to deserving this kind of treatment. It is all so viciously convoluted that I cannot get a stable perspective on it. the only way these criminals in uniform can do anything more diabolical to me would be to chain me to the wall and I am sure they would if they thought they could get away with it. Their intransigence seems to be the result of fundamental dissociation with concepts of typical human rights. The entire apparatus is a testimony to their beliefs about their own behavior but might does not make them right. They are very much wrong.

Several staff members appear in the hall by the outer door. The door powers up and slides to the side. A tall gangly guard who is carrying a stick comes in and stands in the sally port. He is followed by a short stocky fellow wearing a blue shirt and tie. Another guard stands at the door with a radio in one hand and a stick in the other. The short casually dressed guy is looking all around the cell and then looks at Powers.

CASE MANAGER: Powers, I'm your case manager. You are now housed in the ADX control unit for a term of sixty months. The way you get credit for each month is to obey all institutional rules and orders and to appear for your team meeting each month. You still have over three years of disciplinary segregation pending, so we are going to continue that, which means you will not have a TV, telephone calls, or commissary for that period.

POWERS: Hold up. Are you telling me that you expect me to sit in this nasty ass cell for the next three years with nothing? I don't think that is going to work for me or for you.

CASE MANAGER: You must not realize where you are. This is the end of the line. You are here because you escaped from a secure Bureau facility. You embarrassed the Bureau of Prisons, and now you are going to pay the price for having done so. If you want to cooperate, that's good; if not, that's good too. Making threats against your case manager is not going to help you.

POWERS: I'm telling you that you're a fool if you think I'm going to sit here on the concrete and twiddle my thumbs for the next three years. That DS time is not supposed to follow me here, and you know it. You don't know the facts and circumstances of the escape. I already got forty-five months added onto my sentence together with all of the DHO sanctions. And why shouldn't I get credit for the last two years I spent in the hole at Lewisburg.

CASE MANAGER: You only get credit when you maintain clear conduct, and you incurred numerous incident reports. Our Warden has made it clear that he wants you to continue your DS time, and I cannot overrule him even if I was favor of giving you a break, which I am not. So, we will get you some cleaning supplies and your other issue during regular rounds. Otherwise, I will see you next month. I strongly suggest you don't give my staff any trouble.

POWERS: Yeah, don't bet on it.

Some people say, "If I could go back and do it all again, I wouldn't change a thing." Well, I would change just about everything! The stark and solitary experience at the ADX supermax provided me with a lot of time and opportunity for reflection. I was mad with myself more than I was mad at anyone else because I am the one who was stupid enough to commit federal crimes. And for what? It certainly did not put me over the top. It was all for peanuts. I had had legitimate opportunities, but I did not know how to go about making the most of them.

One of the things that always struck me hard in the heart was what I had inadvertently done to my loved ones. I had no idea what I was doing or what the results would be, and they were disastrous. I had put myself, my loved ones, and all of us futures in jeopardy. I wanted to live large, be a big shot, have money to throw around. Money, yeah, money. I was an asshole, pure and simple. My ignorance and selfishness were intense and quite pronounced. To find I did not have it all under control the way I thought or in any discernable way whatsoever-- was a trauma I would rather have avoided.

> *It is a beautiful sunny day in Florida. My wife is at school, and I am getting prepared to rob a bank. I have a disguise that I am putting on so I will not be readily identified. I will wear a false beard, an oversized suit with regular clothing under-neath, and a hat and sunglasses. I will carry a satchel and hand a note about the size of a check to the teller. I will use a stolen car to drive to the bank and, after leaving the bank, I will drive it to a nearby parking lot and leave it. Hopefully I will be home before my wife gets there everything goes as planned and I get away with a stack of cash. I make it home with time to spare, and I am taking off my fake beard when my wife suddenly appears at the bedroom door. She sees the money on the bed, and she sees me with half a false beard on my face. I give her a story about using a disguise to take out a loan, but she is suspicious. When the news comes on later that evening, she sees a crime stoppers segment that shows me walking across the bank with a satchel in my hand. She now knew what had happened, so I went ahead and confessed to her. She was frightened but finally agreed to keep everything confidential. Well, that worked out for about two weeks--until we had an argument, and she began to make phone calls.*

The cell has nothing going on. There is nothing to do. Powers has been pacing back and forth. He has found that if he steps up onto the concrete bunk and walks to the corner, he can get an extra step in. He has received a laundry bag with clothing and linen and toiletries inside, and he has cleaned the cell thoroughly. He is wearing a fresh pair of socks and boxer shorts. He hears a voice coming through the vent cover over the light: "Yo, Powers, use your toilet paper roll to blow the water out of your sink drain so we can talk." Powers goes ahead and sets the roll over the drain in the sink and blows hard, and this pushes the water out of the J-channel in the sink's drain.

POWERS: (into the toilet paper tube) Yeah, what's up?

JOKER: They call me Joker. Where are you coming in from?

POWERS: Lewisburg, but you probably already know that.

JOKER: Yeah, we heard you were on your way. Those lames at Lewisburg didn't carry the ball like they were supposed to.

POWERS: What is that supposed to mean?

JOKER: They didn't kill you. They were supposed to kill you.

POWERS: They had their chance. It didn't go quite how they thought it would.

JOKER: We will get to you and get it done eventually. Could be sooner, could be later, but you are in our space now. They sent you here to get you killed.

POWERS: I know it, but I am not about to go down without putting up a good fight.

JOKER: You're a dead man, Powers.

POWERS: Yeah, I know it. Hopefully I get to take one of you punks with me.

Generally speaking, prisons and jails are dangerous places. It is mostly violent gangs, homosexuality, drug use, gambling and boredom. There is absolutely nothing good that goes on. Prisoners get beat up, extorted, raped, stabbed, and killed all the time. Anyone who tries to detach from a criminal mentality is going to be caught between the proverbial rock and a hard place. It is hard enough to keep hope alive; it is harder still to engage a course of change; and it is hardest of all to maintain personal dignity. It is not a good scene and anyone who has half a brain will do whatever they can do to avoid it in the first place. There is very little, if any, fulfillment or value in spending years under the kinds of influences that prisons and jails typically feature.

The Other Prisoners

THE prisoners at ADX get word through the grapevine about who is coming and going. It is amazing how much accurate information they can glean from such limited resources. They already know who I am and why I am here. My life is in serious danger no matter where I am. They already tried to take me out at USP Lewisburg. Two "hitters" had been detailed to purposely go into the segregated housing unit for the express purpose of killing me. We were heading to the recreation area, going down the stairs in G-unit, when they made their move. Luckily, I was a little faster and a little smarter. Later on, an orderly took a swipe at my neck with a razor blade and caught the side of my face. These events occurred while I was under administrative confinement--that is, solitary confinement--and proving that where there is a will, there is a way.

My enemies are the heaviest of heavy gang members, and Bureau of Prisons staff might be willing to facilitate them to some degree. I have seen prisoners who were handcuffed and being escorted by guards get jumped by prisoners who had jimmied their doors. The outer doors in the control unit are not supposed to open while the inner doors are open, but it already happened yesterday afternoon while the guards were handing out supplies. I have been using a braided piece of sheet to tie the bottom of the sally port door to the bars so it cannot be readily opened. A couple of the guards have warned me about it, but I have to consider my safety to be paramount to their concerns.

But if one or more prisoners are able to breech the outer door, a strip of sheet is not going to stop them. For all I know they could have a flammable liquid they could throw in on me or an explosive device they could roll under the door. They have been steadily talking and, presumably, plotting. There is virtually nothing for me to fight back with. Most of them likely have access to weapons of one kind or another. They will carry a 5- or 6-inch homemade knife, a "shank," up their ass. They can saw a knife out of metal with nothing more than a string! Given enough time, they will come up with something. It is inconceivable to them that I am housed in the same unit with them.

Nearly every prisoner who is confined in the control unit has either killed another prisoner or has committed a serious assault on staff. I was sent here because I escaped from a secure prison and, hence, embarrassed the Bureau of Prisons. The guards want everything to run as smoothly as possible, so they tend to cater to the shot callers. A bit earlier, a guard came onto the range and went into one of the cells downrange. He remained in the sally port for a good while, talking to one of the highest-ranking members of the Aryan Brotherhood prison gang. I could not hear what he was saying but it sounded like I heard my name come up. This causes me a lot of anxiety.

So, Powers is trying to rest his head. He is kicking back on the bunk, nearly asleep, when he feels a moist sensation on the back of his head accompanied with a putrid smell. He touches at the back of his head and jumps up to look at the wall where his head had rested. There is a yellowish-brown substance coming through a crack near the ceiling. It is a foul mixture of shit and piss that is being poured through the crack in the wall from above. He stands back and watches with a resigned disgust as the mixture of excrement runs off of the bunk and forms a puddle on the floor.

> *Everyone has a sense of right and wrong, and human life is full of choices between the two. The main problem is that doing the wrong thing is usually easier or safer or more expedient. Sometimes we are influenced in our choices by facts and circumstances that are compelling. We make a million choices every day, but most of them we make out of habit. There are forces of life and death that are nearly impossible to deny. To be your own person and to go your own way means you must be ever more conscious of the choices you make: you must be sure they are your own. The consequences might be severe, but the reward is your enhanced sense of integrity and decency as a human being. No one can take that away from you.*

Just as Powers has begun to fall asleep after a couple of hours of cleaning and disinfecting and showering some passing guard pauses to strike the outer door with the butt end of his night stick. It sounds like gunshots inside the concrete cell. Powers is upset about it, but he is too tired to get up again. He thinks about all the little techniques the staff members have at their disposal to make his time that much harder. He realizes that his troubles not only involve the other prisoners, but also involve the staff members on the unit. They have already put small stones into mashed potatoes and soup on the meal trays one of which chipped a front tooth. For several days they had denied him a roll of toilet paper and, when his toilet plugged from trying to flush a washcloth, they left it plugged for several more days... Powers finally drifts off into a release from his physical reality.

> *The cell doors open after 4:00 p.m. count and I put my shoes on. I have a bad feeling in the pit of my stomach. It is almost chow time, and I am hungry, but there are more important*

matters to deal with. just then, four prisoners book past my cell and enter the cell of my next-door neighbor. It sounds like a cell fight banging and clanging noises. I go to his assistance, but one of the attackers leaps from the cell and stabs at me with a shank. I jump back into my cell and grab my lock and belt strap and go back out onto the catwalk. I begin to holler, and the pack of attackers takes off toward the far stairwell. My neighbor stumbles out of his cell. His eyes are wide with fear and glassy. Arterial blood is spraying from his neck. He grabs for me with both hands and says, "John, help me." The front of his shirt is drenched with blood and a spurt of blood from a deep gash in the side of his neck hits me in the face. I try to stop the bleeding by sticking my thumb into his neck. We get about ten steps down the range, and he falls unconscious. I pick him up and get him over my shoulder and carry him down the five flight of stairs.

The dreams are vivid and real, the kind that affect Powers even after he is awake. It is as though his mind comes loose from his body. It is like the layers of time and space are stripped away like calendar pages being flipped backwards. There is more than a primal fear or desire at work; it is some element of the soul that has broken off and is trying to float away. It makes Powers want to kill himself. It makes him smell blood. It makes him question everything about himself. It makes him doubt the merits of existence. It makes him sweat, makes his heart palpitate, makes him feel trapped.

The same general dream happens: Powers is in some solitary place in an isolated area of a prison. He is studying or writing when he notices certain gang members taking up positions around him. They close in quickly, brandish weapons, and begin the attack. Powers fights for his life, using anything and everything around him to his advantage. He climbs pipes, he outruns them, he uses books to block their weapons. The fights can last for a long time, and Powers often wakes up in a sweat, feeling exhausted. He hates these dreams but can do nothing to stop them from coming. The fact is my neighbor was also one of the few men I considered to be a friend. His name was Eddie, and he was a good-hearted dude. He had been named in a dry heroin conspiracy (that is, no drugs found) and given a lengthy term of imprisonment. He was a first-time offender who had a wife and two little girls. The gang members had come to him earlier that morning with an ultimatum: "Either you send this amount of money to this address by this time next week, or we will murder you." It was simple and direct, and Eddie did not know what to do.

Being brand new a "fish" to the prison experience, not knowing who he could trust and who he could not trust, and being shocked and frightened by the threat, Eddie made a big mistake. He went to other prisoners and tried to get them to help him. What he did not realize was that these other prisoners were part of the same gang that was terrorizing him. The shot-callers did not like this and decided to make a statement, so they came back that same afternoon and knifed him. He was stabbed 13 times in his chest, neck, and back. It was a brutal and senseless murder, and it affected me profoundly.

> *It is a surreal scene. I am locked inside a holding cell, waiting for someone to tell me what is going on. I hear noise in the hallway and go to the door. They are wheeling Eddie out on a stretcher. he seems to be at peace. I keep going to the drinking fountain to wash blood off of me. My hair and face and clothing is matted with dried blood. My own wounds are bleeding, but this has not caused me to be covered from head to toe with blood! it is Eddie's blood. I keep on trying to wash it off with water from the drinking fountain. There is now watery blood all over the fountain and the floor near the fountain. it will not wash out! I can smell it and taste it. there is no way to get it out of my mind....*

The F.B.I. and prison officials came to me and asked me to help them. They told me that these same gang members had been robbing, raping, and murdering prisoners left and right. They said nobody wanted to cooperate. They said that because I intervened, my own life was now in danger. They said I would have to remain locked up in the segregation unit until they completed their investigation. They said that if I helped them, they would help me. They said I would be moved to a decent prison and would be eligible for a sentence reduction. I was reluctant and told them I needed time to think about it.

I am in the cell, walking back and forth, thinking about what had happened. Suddenly the lead shot caller for the gang is at my cell door, standing there, looking in at me. He places his head down by the food hatch and motions to me to come closer. I know him from my days at Leavenworth, and I have never liked him. I begin to wonder how he is allowed to be at my cell door. There is a young guard over by the front who is waiting for him. He finally says, "You tell on my boys, and I will chop your fucking head off." I leap forward and try to stick my fingers into his eyes, and he jumps away. "You're a dead man, Powers. I am going to cut your head off and roll it down the range."

After that, I said I needed to talk to a lieutenant. It took a while before anyone came around. The next day they pulled me back out and circled around while I told them what had transpired. I also told them that I had decided that I had no choice but to go ahead and cooperate. The F.B.I. took down my statement while other staff members went in and out of the room. When it was time to go, I was escorted all the way out to a van that was waiting in the transport garage. As we drove away, I thought that I was never so glad to be away from a place.

> *It is my first day of junior high school. I go into the bathroom on the first floor. There are a bunch of students in there and I smell cigarette smoke. Someone I do not know asks me to stand by the garbage can and watch for any teachers who might bust them for smoking. I stand there and watch, but I do not know what exactly I am watching for. There are several boys lighting up in the back by the urinals. just as I look back toward the door, a little guy in a yellow shirt blasts past me and begins to grab those who is smoking. He is the vice principal. He gives me a look and I slide on out of there. It is rather obvious they made a bad choice when they selected me to be their lookout.*

Protective Custody

MY decision to cooperate with the F.B.I. automatically made me a "rat" in the minds of those who would prefer to keep their misdeeds concealed. It also made me a direct target of the most powerful and violent prison gang in the federal prison system, the Aryan Brotherhood. I had already been told by federal agents and prosecutors that there was a contract on my life. Apparently, the Aryan Brotherhood was in league with the Mexican Mafia, and this meant that the contract could be executed by virtually anyone in the system. They explained that I would need to be placed in a protective custody program.

Now, I have never been a "rat." To me, a rat is someone who is involved in criminal activities with others, gets busted, and tells on everyone in order to get him or herself out of trouble. Someone who witnesses a criminal act and intervenes and later decides to cooperate is not typically considered to be a rat. In any case, prison gang members do not make these distinctions. They somehow believe they can intimidate, harm, or kill potential witnesses against them. It is part of their overall game plan as an organized criminal enterprise. Had their shot-caller not appeared at my cell front to threaten me, I most likely would not have decided to cooperate. They left me no choice.

To make a long story short, I was bounced around from one spot to another. The protective custody was being moved from one prison to another, being kept in isolation cells, and being deprived of my property and privileges. It was hell-on-wheels, but there was nothing I could do to change it. The worst part was when I would break out in a cold sweat and think I was having a heart attack. I would have to lie down and look at the ceiling and wait to die. If a door slammed somewhere, I would have a serious startle response that would last for hours and hours. This is also when the dreams began. Sometimes I would become dissociated with the immediate reality and have flashbacks of the murder.

It was during these times that I began to consider suicide as an option. The only thing that kept me going was the prosecutor's promise of a sentence reduction. I wanted to go home. I wanted to make things up to my loved ones while I still could. They had told me that this was my ticket out, and I kept wondering what was taking them so long. There was no one who kept contact with me; no one to help me deal with any of it. I was simply considered to be a witness-in waiting while they came up to speed on the prosecution. I took to making and drinking prison-made wine called "hooch" that I made with food items like fruit, potatoes, bread, and sugar packets.

The day finally arrived when the U.S. Marshals showed up to get me. It was like a dark night had finally given way to the dawn. We rode to the airport in a late model SUV; they stopped to buy me a meal at McDonald's; they even took me on a commercial flight. I remember a woman who was struggling to place something into an overhead compartment. I went to help her but the chain around me waist and the handcuffs prevented me from doing so. I was more tied up than she! Being suddenly among the people of the outside world was comforting. No one seemed to pay much attention to the two men in suitcoats who kept a handcuffed man between them. A stewardess even brought earphones and I watched the movie "Twins." It was somewhat of a teaser, though, because within a couple of hours I was back inside a holding cell.

The trial was uneventful. I was brought in last--probably to put the cap on the prosecution's case. It was not anything that I enjoyed doing, but it had to be done. I had no bad feelings against the men on trial. If anything, I felt sorry for them in a way that is hard to describe. But they had murdered Eddie for nothing, and they did it right in my face. When I came to my friend's assistance, I myself had been assaulted. After that, they had tried to have me killed by publicizing a contract on my life throughout the federal prison system. My only choice was to stand against them. It was my duty if I wanted to maintain my dignity as a human being.

After the trial I was taken to another federal prison that is specifically used for federal witnesses. There were a lot of well-known mobsters, drug kingpins, and others who had agreed to cooperate with the government. It was a strange place where the prisoners themselves had a lot of leverage and special privileges, Yet I was there a short time when I began to have some fairly severe symptoms. One guy patted me on the shoulder in what he thought was a friendly gesture, and I whirled around and struck him before I knew what I was doing. I barely even knew the dude! Of course, this got me tossed into the small and nicely appointed segregation unit there. I once again began to have nightmares and flashbacks and dissociative episodes. It came to the point where I had to ask to see a psychologist.

*There is no outdoor recreation. It is only a large concrete room
with brown block walls and beams overhead. One corner of the
roof is cut away and a wire mesh has been installed. The
sunlight comes down through this opening and splays across
the concrete. A black mud wasp lands on the ledge and begins
an aggressive search. It looks like Darth Vader, and it has a
lethal demeanor. It tries to get under a flat piece of metal and a*

fat brown spider emerges from the other end. The wasp attacks
without even a millisecond of delay. The chunky brown spider is
a fighter! It is beneath the wasp, biting at its midsection while
the wasp stings repeatedly and begins biting with hydraulic
jaws. The spider is eventually defeated in this epic battle, and
the wasp carries pieces to its nest in the rafters... but the next
day, the wasp is on the concrete floor beneath the nest--dead as
a doornail.

PSYCHOLOGIST: You wanted to see me, so here I am. What's going on with you?

POWERS: Weird stuff, man. I have been having panic attacks and vivid dreams and strange sensations like I can smell blood or have blood on me that I can't wash off. One time it looked like a puddle of blood on the floor but was only a shadow. I seem to be having anxiety and I startle easily. I've been thinking about death a lot.

PSYCHOLOGIST: Are you suicidal?

POWERS: I don't think I am.

PSYCHOLOGIST: Well, do you have a plan?

POWERS: To commit suicide? No.

PSYCHOLOGIST: From what I hear, you have been somewhat reclusive. Do you know when you will be coming out of segregation?

POWERS: I can go any time, I guess. But I told them I want to stay here until I can figure out what is going on with me. There is something wrong with me.

PSYCHOLOGIST: You could have PTSD. People do have reactions to traumatic events that mess with their mental functions. What you are describing are classic symptoms of PTSD. Can you begin to keep a record of when these things are happening? How often? I can't make a diagnosis without sufficient information.

And so, I waited about 4 years for the government to do its part and cut me loose. When I found out that it had all been a lie, I fell apart, got myself back together in a different way, and began to plan another way out. I kept on thinking that I had a perfect right to escape under the circumstances. It was
beyond belief that after all I had been through that there would be no relief forthcoming. I had attempted to save Eddie's life, had been assaulted in the process, had been threatened, had to go into protective custody, contracted PTSD, lost all of my personal possessions, and a lot more and now I was being left high and dry? It was too much.

It is a Friday evening the designated day for me to make my escape. I have made a realistic dummy that is in the bed. I have my little pack of protein bars, tape, FedEx boxes, nail clippers, sewing kit, and water bottle. I go onto the recreation yard and stay out there. When everyone else goes inside, I drop down into a drainage grate and pull the cover over me. The guards inside lock down the cells. there is no alarm, so I know they did not discover the dummy. after a while, I come out and proceed to climb onto the roof. I throw my pack over the first security fence, and it lands in between the fences. then, I get a good run across the rooftop and leap out as far as I can leap. I clear the top of the razor wire and land between the fences with a heavy thud. no alarms sound. the night is still. I tape the FedEx boxes around my arms and legs and begin climbing through the multiple rolls of razor wire. I make it to the top of the outer security fence and jump down onto free ground.

Like a true dummy, I decide to go see some members of my family. It is obviously what law enforcement expected me to do, for they tapped everyone's telephones. Before long there is a big manhunt under way, and I am the subject of it. I got away only to turn right around and go back again. This time they caught me and brought me right on back to prison. Except now I was in far worse shape than ever because I had more time added onto my sentences and was designated to the supermax as punishment for having escaped my captors. Now I was hated by everyone albeit for different reasons all around, and I was stuck in the lowest place under the most adverse circumstances imaginable.

Back Inside Cell 208

THE ADX is designed to incapacitate prisoners who are considered to be the worst of the worst. It is a hardline approach with no frills. The staff is hardboiled and no nonsense. Once every couple of weeks the administrative staff walks the ranges. As soon as they come through the gate, a staff member yells: "Warden on the range!" They come by wearing suits or short sleeved shirts and ties. They only pause at each cell for a moment before moving on to the next cell. Sometimes the captain will give rookie guards a tour of the control unit. I was by the door in the recreation area one day when I heard him giving them a speech:

> *The ADX is unlike any other prison in the system. The inmates who are sent here are the most dangerous inmates in the system. They have proven they cannot be confined in any of our one-hundred and twenty some odd facilities. They have engaged in acts of terrorism, mass murder, organized crime, and other unspeakable acts. These are not your average criminals: they are devious and ruthless and, yes, evil. Do not let them fool you! Our mission is to contain that evil, so it does not spread. they will try you, test you, and push your buttons. They are master manipulators. Remember that it is their job to get away with everything they can, and it is your job to catch them. And should you begin to feel sympathy for them, remember that they do not feel pain or empathy or emotions like ordinary human beings do. these are psychopaths and sociopaths. They will stab you through the bars and stand there laughing while you bleed out. Whatever happened to them to make them this way is not our concern. Our only concern is to incapacitate them.*

The guards have been instructed to keep a close eye on Powers lest he find some way to escape. They are paranoid about the possibility. Therefore, they make it a point to go inside his cell every day to shake it down. They check the bars by banging on them with rubber mallet; they check the window for signs of digging, cutting, or sawing; they pound around on the walls and ceiling to make sure there are no false panels. They listen in via the intercom in the sally port for any irregular sounds. There is no camera in the cell, though.

Every time Powers is taken out of cell 208, he is first strip searched, then chained up, then patted down in the hallway outside the cell, and then waned with a metal detector. He is watched more closely than the World Trade Center bomber, who

21

happens to be in the same facility. At one point the guards confiscate the braided piece of sheet Powers uses to tie the inner door and claim it is a hazardous tool escape equipment. They write him an incident report, which requires Powers to appear at a hearing that is conducted by the disciplinary hearing officer

> D.H.O.: (looking at papers) Have a seat. (To guards) Stay in the room, please. (To Powers) Name and number.

> POWERS: Powers, zero-three-two-two-zero-zero-two-eight.

> D.H.O.: You've been given your rights. I see you did not request any witnesses. It says here that you braided together strips torn from a sheet. You are charged with possession of a hazardous tool. How do you plead?

> POWERS: Not guilty.

> D.H.O.: Well, with your escape history, I am going to find you guilty and sanction you to a loss of good time, commissary, visits and property.

> POWERS: Is that all?

> D.H.O.: You can appeal my decision, if you choose, under the administrative remedies program statement.

I am trying to make it the best way I know how. I study and write and exercise. I have begun to practice yoga meditation through a correspondence course. The black mastic around the window makes excellent ear plugs. I save pats of margarine and, when I get enough, put them into a plastic bag and fill it with hot water. The oil then comes to the top, and I put a hole in the bottom of the bag and let the water drain out. The oil I use to make a candle, and I use the candle at night when I meditate. I folded my blanket and use it to sit on while I gaze at the candle and try to clear my mind. Sometimes I hold small pieces of bread over the flame and make toast.

There are a couple of exceedingly good men who work as chaplains here. They have helped me a great deal by being friendly toward me and by bringing me books. I am of the opinion that I need to take a close look at myself and figure out what needs to be changed. It is the hardest thing for me to see myself the way others see me or to accept that there are defects in my personal character, but there are. The spiritual disciplines seem to promote that kind of insight and understanding. It is like layers and layers of realization. One thing I know is that there is always an opportunity for some degree of redemption.

POWERS: (to Chaplain) Do you think a person can be so far off the path that he has no redeemable qualities whatsoever?

CHAPLAIN: Anyone can turn his life around if he truly wants to. It is a matter of determination, instruction and discipline. I am not in a position to judge anyone.

POWERS: But how can a man see the poor shape he is in if he is effectively blind to his own condition?

CHAPLAIN: The breakthroughs or insights usually come as the result of some major emotional turbulence. At that point, they cry out for God's help, and God begins to help them.

POWERS: Then what or who is God? Is it some kind of existential energy?

CHAPLAIN: God is beyond human comprehension. The best we can do is to look to Jesus, the Christ, for understanding. One of the greatest men of God once said, "Sit quietly in your cell and your cell will teach you everything." Of course, their cells were worse than yours is here, and they went into them voluntarily.

There are many people whose thinking, and behavior is so crooked that they must be removed from society for a time. But although people who commit certain kinds of crime must be confined, there is no reason to make them even worse off. The very fact of being chained and placed into cages is repugnant to notions of any civilized society. There is not a good plan for the correction of aberrant behavior. Unfortunately, no one has any good answers. There is only so far that anyone can go in terms of motivating any human being to alter his or her behavior, and it is hard work...there are those who are already confined who have become so decrepit in their character that they will never be able to adjust to societal standards. This does not mean they are incorrigible per se; it only means that society has yet to develop viable methods for inducing people to stay within the boundaries of the law. Harsh punishment does not work and reforming a person's character is difficult at best.

There are noises coming from down the range. Someone is hollering. It is impossible for me to make out what is going on. I hear the electronically controlled gates opening somewhere up front. Then I hear radios squawking and keys jangling. It sounds like an army coming up the stairs. The guards run past my cell. One of them yells to another to go get a stretcher. There is a lot of commotion. After what seems like a long time, they carry a prisoner who is unconscious and on a stretcher past my cell. Everything has gone eerily quiet. I have no way to know what happened, but it makes things more complicated.

I begin to pace back and forth again. A large part of my day is spent pacing. I must put in some serious mileage. Lately I have noticed that the shower water gets hotter at night, so I have taken to showering at 1:00 or 2:00 a.m. I put newspaper over the opening to hold the steam inside the stainless-steel upright box, and I sit down inside with my legs folded. The water is a comfort to me. One time I used the transparent plastic shower curtain to form a barrier around the bottom of the shower so I could take a bath. I was able to shift my body so that my legs were going up the wall and my head was under the water. It was actually quite deep in there. But I did not think about what would happen if I stood up. Well, my body weight had held the plastic in place and now there was nothing to hold it. The barrier gave way and a substantial wave of water burst forth and flooded my cell and part of the range.

The monotony is terrible! I finally decided to build a basketball court. I used paper that I rolled up tightly into a tube for the rim and tied that to a flattened-out milk carton and then used toothpaste to stick it to the bulkhead by the sally port. I then made a ball of toilet paper and covered it with a sock. Now I am able to shoot baskets from around the cell. It is a lot of fun, and I get a lot of exercise. The main game I play I call "Beat the Shower." When I hit the button inside the shower, the shower runs for something over a minute. During that time I have to make as many shots as I can. But I can only take a layup after I have hit a shot from behind the imaginary line by the back wall where the edge of the shower sticks out.

Ideas about how to structure my time are coming to me. I have a list of sixteen possible activities. So, it is a matter of time management when there is too much as opposed to too little time on your hands. I am a time engineer. I have the cage and time. The day is divided into meal times and count times that form three blocks of time: morning, afternoon, and evening. Since the morning seems the best time for exercise related activities, I schedule those in on that block. The afternoon, then is for study related matters. And the evening block is for passive leisure time, such as drawing or leisure reading or meditation. My plan also calls for 15-minute segments of activity followed by a break. Then I can also rearrange the activities within any block of time to mix it up a bit.

It is snowing heavily. Powers is an 8 years old and is trying to keep up with the older kids. They are deep in the woods and, by all accounts, lost. They continue to trudge along through heavy snow, and their footprints disappear almost as soon as they are made. The older boys pull ahead, and powers stops to rest. The snow storm increases and comes down in blankets. Powers does not know which way the others have gone. He is now effectively separated from them, and it is getting dark. He is too fatigued to do much. His feeble calls go unanswered. He is now alone. He finds a corpse of smallish evergreens and craws into the relative shelter beneath them. It is warm and comfortable there. He is not panicked or even worried all that much. He is tired and lies down. Just as he is falling into a deep sleep there are rescuers who are blowing horns and shouting. He raises up and calls back, but his voice doesn't carry too far. Now he is panicked. He keeps trying to respond but his voice will not carry. Finally, the searchers come close enough to find him, and they carry him out.

When the chances of relief are zero, it is easy to lose a grip on hope. It is a foul feeling an empty twisting and gnawing in the pit of the stomach. When the situation is not going to be resolved but, instead is going to be extended in perpetuity, the depth and degree of despair is hard to describe. When some people hold other people captive and keep them inside carefully monitored and controlled cages, the potential for abuse becomes a pronounced reality. There are times and places in life where the dreams of the future
are blank. This is the void that sits at the center of the soul. It is so deep and so dark that it seems endless.

Trying to Stay Good

SO much of this is unnecessary. Think about the monumental task of keeping so many people in cages. Start with the facilities, their designs and expense. Then there are all of the standard utilities that must be provided and maintained. Then there is the need for staff, which includes medical, dental, facilities, administrative, secretarial, and correctional. Think of their salaries, benefits, and retirement plans. Then there are all the furnishings and supplies such as desks, toilet paper, ink cartridges whatever. Then comes the costs of food and food services, medical supplies and prescription drugs, clothing and hygiene items, radios and security equipment, and all kinds of additional and incidental expenses.

Now think about how difficult it is to keep the people who in cages alive, secure, and manageable. They have to be cared for in ways that are much different from the care of animals kept in cages at zoos. Human beings have rights; they have needs that go far beyond the need for food and water; they are much more complicated. The psychological component alone is nearly impossible to fathom. By any measure, keeping human beings in cages is a gigantic responsibility especially when the outcome tends to generate an even greater problem than the one it hoped to solve. The biggest cost is the loss of human potential as a by-product of forced incapacitation. There are not many prisoners who emerge from the cage in better shape than when they went in.

> PSYCHOLOGIST: Got your cop-out. You weren't too specific about what is going on.

> POWERS: (indicating guards) Can we talk outside their presence?

> PSYCHOLOGIST: Can't do that. They have to be present per policy.

> POWERS: What about confidentiality and all that?

> PSYCHOLOGIST: If you want to talk to me you are going to have to forget about confidentiality. We are all correctional officers first even the chaplains so keep that in mind. I don't have a lot of time, so what is you want?

> POWERS: Well, it's weird stuff that's going on: dreams, flashbacks, strange feelings and sensations and--

PSYCHOLOGIST: Everyone has strange dreams now and then. Given your history, it doesn't surprise me.

POWERS: What does that mean?

PSYCHOLOGIST: It means you have had some traumatic events, but nothing that is outside the ordinary. And remember, too that you brought most of it upon yourself.

POWERS: Wow. Thanks for all your good input. I feel so much better now.

One good thing about being in solitary confinement is the opportunity to do a lot of thinking. In the silence and quietude, memories rise to the surface of my mind. A sound, a smell, perhaps a position or posture can trigger them, and the past becomes the present. Over the weeks and months and years, the isolated mind takes on new powers of concentration, insight, and understanding. It breaks free from its moorings and begins to sail off into un-charted waters. This can have both good and poor results; it all depends on whether the new course is purposeful or haphazard. One thing is for certain: the mind is able to generate alternative realities.

One of the things I have created for myself is an imaginary family. I have taken them all from newspapers and magazines, and they are pasted to the wall, looking at me. My dad is a studious and handsome devil who works as an engineer at an aerospace company. He has blue eyes and salt-and-pepper hair and is in his mid-50s. My mom is a shapely woman with long auburn hair and a beautiful smile. She works as a yoga instructor and owns a studio in town. My sister is my paternal twin. She is two minutes older than I am, and we are both 17 years old. We both have our driver's licenses and tool around in beaters. I have a Toyota Corolla and my sister has a Chevy Camaro. We live in nice home that is surrounded by woods and has a lot of deck space.

These are people I can talk to and love. Occasionally I help my mom out at her yoga studio; my sister and I are close but somehow always manage to seem distant; my dad is usually at work but comes out to shoot some hoops with me now and then. We keep in contact throughout the day by cellphone (I use an empty deodorant container to mimic one). I have a fairly rigid schedule each day. I work part time in the morning, go to school in the afternoon, and have leisure time activities in the evening. On the weekends I can sleep in, lounge around, and do other things or nothing, my choice.

*It is impossible to adequately describe the feelings of being so
vitally separated from family, friends and freedom. and on top
of that, to be isolated from any other human beings and left to
the ravages of silence and time and boredom. To me this is a
torture that is unlike any other because the emotional pain
becomes sharper each day and never goes away. Recently, I
have taken to yelling and screaming at the top of my lungs just
to get it out. The other day a small bird landed on the window
ledge outside and pecked around before taking off again. I
wanted him to stay for a while so I could look at him and talk to
him. The loneliness is what gets me down. I need someone to
love me and to listen to me and to understand me. It is as if,
without others to validate me, I do not really exist. my entire
life is now a questionable thing that has no apparent answers. I
am alone.*

Prior to his trial for the escape Powers was diagnosed with PTSD by two
psychologists and two psychiatrists. After he was found guilty, the Federal Bureau
of Prisons placed him in the ADX's control unit. Part of the regulations concerning
the control unit stated, if effect, that a prisoner with a serious mental health
disorder could not be placed in the control unit. So prior to the transfer, the FBOP
had Powers diagnosed by one of its own psychologists. Not surprisingly, that
psychologist found that Powers was perfectly fine and ordered his medication for
PTSD to be discontinued. This technique allowed the FBOP to effectively skirt its
own rules while denying proper treatment for mental disorders. Powers is not the
only prisoner in the ADX control unit who has a mental disorder and is being
denied proper treatment.

A phalanx of guards comes onto the range. It is a lot of activity all of a sudden.
They have trash cans, plastic bags, carts, metal detectors and more. They are
dressed in SWAT type clothing and snap on rubber gloves. They begin at the front
and strip search each prisoner before removing him from the cell. They wave a
metal detector over them and pat search. Each prisoner is taken to a designated
holding area and locked in while the cells are being torn up. It is not long before
they come to my cell and take me out. I see a lot of stuff being piled up in the
hallway. Boxes, bags and mattresses are being thrown onto carts and wheeled up
front for x-rays. They go into my cell and, after a minute or two, one of them
comes out with my basketball hoop and shows it to another guard. He tears it apart
and throws it into the trash.

*I am walking among the debris, looking down and around and
wondering why they tore up my family. They are all gone from
their places as if some horrible event happened. I know they are
gone forever because I am unable to replace them. My comb is
floating in the toilet, and there are margarine pats mushed into
my legal papers. Even the picture of Jesus I got from an eastern
orthodox book has been trashed. It looks like a bomb went off
inside the cell. I am pissed and stunned and sad all at once. I
feel some kind of explosive rage building up inside of me, but I
cannot express it. This creates even more frustration. From the
remnants of the margarine, I build a candle. I use a piece of
torn newspaper to make a flame from the lighter in the wall. I
take a piece of a paperclip they did not find and heat it until it
is bright red. Then I press it against my skin. it sizzles, pops and
smells funny. I do the same thing over and over until I have
deep burned all over my legs and belly.*

The administration frowns on prisoners who demonstrate creativity. To encourage
such a thing would go against the goal of forced idleness and learned helplessness.
One of the main purposes of solitary confinement is to dumb prisoners down.
Those prisoners who sit around all day watching TV, gossiping about others,
jacking off and thinking about criminal events do become lethargic and fall into a
mental stupor. When I look out the window, all I see is a brick wall. It is planned
this way. There are no colors anywhere in the
cells or hallways. Everything is intentionally flat and bland and boring.

Any kind of hobby craft or artwork is restricted. A host and variety of publications
are banned even down to receiving colored paper. And communication with the
outside world is virtually non-existent. There is not a ball, a mat, or a jump rope in
the recreation areas only concrete and steel. The only item that is issued to occupy
the mind is a TV set, and the only content is murder and mayhem. I am glad I do
not have one. These other prisoner most of them are electronically shackled to
what I refer to as the dummy box.

*Any person who ends up on the low side of life has experienced
at least one life changing event that happened at an early age.
Someone did something to them that stuck with them and
became a controlling factor in their lives. It is not an excuse,
but it is a cause. Most prisoners have been the victims of crime*

29

themselves. Those who study such things know this. yet, even
with the knowledge of what constitutes the cause of crime, the
focus remains on the effect of crime. This is why imprisonment
as a remedy does not work. It addresses the effect while
ignoring the cause.

It is getting darker outside. I realize this as I come out of some foggy state of mind that remembers too much. The cell is still in disarray as it was before I drifted, and the candle has gone out. I do not want to move. I look at what I have done to myself and somehow I feel better about my situation. I get up and hide the wire again. Little by little, I begin to salvage whatever can be salvaged. I use the sticky part of an envelope to put the crumpled Jesus picture back in place. This is one of those moments in time when I have gone beyond the thoughts and emotions that tormented me.

The Spider's Web

THERE is a spider at the top of the bars in the sally port, and it has made a threadbare web. It must know what it is doing, but it looks like it ran short on building materials and had to wing it. I admire the way it sits there for hours on end, bored out of its tiny mind, and never complains. The other prisoners have taken to flooding me with mop water and pounding on the walls all night, so I have made a hammock from a sheet I tie between the shower and the bars of the sally port. I was just beginning to fall asleep when I felt something crawling on me. It was the spider, and I do not know which one of us jumped farther....

I am a child and am walking home from first grade. It is a warm and sunny afternoon, and the way home is mostly downhill. It is not too far, but I decide to go another way a shortcut. I cut between the houses and find myself in a backyard with huge trees and lots of long grass. There is a garage back there that has some kind of an enclosure. When I go closer, a little brown and white dog comes out and jumps against the fence holding it in. It is a lovely little dog, lively and anxious to make a friend. I figure out how to open the enclosure and let it out. The little dog runs all around in the high grass as fast as its little legs will carry it. We play a game where the dog comes running at me, I make like I am trying to catch it, and it veers off at the last second and keeps booking.

Most of the prisoners here have other prisoners they associate with by some limited means. They talk and play chess by blowing the water out of the sink drains; they exercise together by going into adjoining recreation areas; they pass small items between cells with a long piece of string called a fishing line. They do not have physical contact, but they have a sense of companionship. They call each other "Homie" and seem to have a lot in common. But due to the peculiarities of both personality and solitary, these relationships sometimes end on a sour note. It is usually some small quirk or paranoid comment that sparks a split. After a time, they usually begin to get along again.

This brings us to what are called "Cell Gangsters." These are prisoners who fill their days by intentionally trying to get other prisoners to hate their guts. They have all kinds of techniques they have honed over their years in seclusion. They move from cell to cell and from range to range often. They typically begin to make small talk to glean as much information as they can about the other prisoners. They then make deals for commissary, dope, pornography and other small items but do not pay up. They rely on the fact that nobody can get to them. And once they are exposed, they begin their roles as Cell Gangsters. They get on the door and make loud threats, reveal information, make things up, and generally do their best to get under the skin of their targets. Sometimes other prisoners will pay them coffee or stamps just to get them to shut up.

A slightly different take exercised by some revolves around homosexual flirtation. These prisoners work long and hard to suck another prisoner into their trap. They connive and scheme, work in one prisoner against another, until they have both a competition and a conflict. All the while they are ingratiating themselves with staff by telling whatever they know or can find out. It is how they do their time. As soon as they get close to a release date, they will do something to extend their stay. It is too difficult to even attempt to figure out why they do what they do.

The recluses are usually the more notorious prisoners like the Shoe bomber, the Unabomber and the Underwear bomber. They rarely, if ever, come out of their cells. They try to get the cells at the far end of the range so that other prisoners are not walking past their cells. They keep their cells darkened all the time by keeping the light off and by covering the back window. They never cause any kind of a disturbance or issue complaints about anything. They also stay completely to themselves and do not talk to anyone. They are not dangerous in the context of prisons, but they are certainly somewhat delusional and perhaps psychotic.

And then there are the "girls." These are those persons who are biologically male but psychologically female. In any prison environment, they provide sex and services such as cleaning cells or washing clothes in exchange for commissary or dope. They use colored pencils and other items for makeup, and they modify their clothing to render it more feminine and stylish. They flaunt their identity because it gets them a lot of attention in places where there are only males. Probably 70 percent of prisoners have had some kind of homosexual interaction at one time or another. At the ADX, the girls gravitate toward the orderly positions so they can stand in the hallway with a broom in hand and
watch a prisoner in the cell masturbate. This is called "bone hawking."

There is yet another kind of sexual activity that has become prevalent in lockdown facilities, and it is called "gunning." A prisoner will watch for certain female staff members to come by his cell. He will call them over on some pretense and, when she looks into the cell, the dude will be standing there naked, pulling his penis to beat the band. It is typically black prisoners and white female staff. As far as anyone can tell, it is a pseudo rape a strange phenomenon that is also considered to be a federal sex offense (though it is likely more of a rebellion against white authority). There are staff members who do not report it. It is impossible to stop and is a source of animosity among the races of prisoners.

> *I am thirteen years old, and it is just after dark on a mid-summer's day. I cut across the lawn and go through the front door of our house. The second I step into the living room, I see a pretty girl who is sitting on the couch, watching tv by herself. I ask who she is, and she tells me she is my brother's girlfriend except he left a while ago and hasn't come back... I go to the fridge and get a couple of cold sodas and go back into the living room and give her one. I sit on the couch beside her, and she tells me she is visiting her father and is in the United States only for the summer. She has a lovely French nose, mouth, and accent. We watch TV for a few minutes, and then she turns to me out of the blue and asks if I know how to French kiss. Her lips are perfect, her tongue is pointed and wet, her breath is root beer. She proceeds to give me instructions and demonstrations until we hear the back door open and notice that my brother has returned.*

No matter what its form, the sex thing seems to be big with the prisoners who are in lockdown 24/7. In the federal prison system, magazines and photographs that show any part of male or female genitalia are strictly prohibited by law. Some prisoners purchase photos from outside dealers that depict scantily clad women but are not technically prohibited. There are some prisoners who masturbate all day long or most of it every day. Other prisoners get items stuck inside their rectums and have to go down to medical to get them removed. Others tie something around their neck and choke themselves while masturbating. The majority of sexual activities occur in secret, so there is no telling what all goes on behind a cell door.

In prison, human beings display the basic characteristics of animal behavior: feeding, breeding, and fighting. None of the reasons for being civilized are present and the individual personality is not refined enough to be viable for that purpose. There is a certain kind of refinement, but this is more along the lines of manipulation and wariness within the prison atmosphere. Most prisoners have low expectations of themselves. They do not have good self-esteem. The values of society are readily cast aside because they are worthless even dangerous inside a prison. It is a completely different world on the inside.

33

Prisoners by and large direct their efforts toward short term gains; that is, any item or activity that makes them feel better about themselves in the moment. They tend to disregard any kind of issue that has no immediate effect on their person. They use a lot of strategies to get what they want: grievances can be filed, staff can be lobbied, information can be traded, rules can be broken, threats or promises can be made, letters can be written, lawsuits can be filed, hunger strikes can be commenced, and if all else fails, violence can be inflicted. Unfortunately, most prisoners are also institutionalized. For too many, their entire outlook on life is only from the perspective of a prison cell.

Every now and then there is a group demonstration that occurs, but these are largely disorganized and somewhat feeble. The prison administrators know how to quell any such disturbance with relative ease. Even when something is terribly wrong and truly needs to be remedied, prison officials will never allow the prisoners to think they have any power. This simply means that any serious protests must be immediately smashed. The ringleaders are rounded up and carted off right away. And once they are out of the picture, the attempt loses its steam. There is usually some show of force followed by a waiting period. Certain detailed adjustments carrots and sticks are meted out during this time. Then when all indications are that there is no more trouble brewing, the prison is gradually brought back up to speed.

> *Powers had been a licensed residential building contractor in the state of Michigan. He ran crews and had some nice projects. But there were pitfalls that he could not avoid: contract issues, tax liens, clients who filed bankruptcy, overdue suppliers bills, theft by employees, and fatigue. Mostly, the trouble was with Powers himself. He was capable but had no formal business training whatsoever. He worked hard but also revealed character flaws. He began to use down payments from one project to pay his expenses on others. He began to lie, cheat and steal. he drank and smoked pot to ease his stress. Things continued to go downhill, and powers turned to crime. He thought he could make one big score and solve all the problems, but this was sheer stupidity.*

The Walls Close In

*The walls seem to be closing in. sometimes I cannot
breathe like there is not enough air coming through. It
panics me, and my head starts swimming in a pool of
nausea. My body feels depleted, sick. It has been days
and days of torment. It is now early in the morning, and I
cannot sleep. I can barely write because my nerves are
on edge and my hand shakes. There has been a lot going
on and I am well past my limits. This cannot continue! I
have tried to do my best but get no help! The people who
surround me and control my life are like foul demons. I
must be in hell. I often wonder if death is the door to life.*

Powers is pacing back and forth. He turns around by the shower, takes a three-step
run, and rams his head into the edge of the steel door casing. Blood spurts from a
gash in his forehead, but he is still conscious. So, he backs up and does it again but
harder this time! During their 3:00 a.m. count, the guards find him lying
unconscious in a pool of blood. They take him to the medical department on a
stretcher. His injuries are too severe to be treated at the prison, so he is eventually
taken to an outside hospital. The doctors attempt to admit Powers for observation,
but the ADX administrators are afraid it is all a ploy to rig an escape, so they order
that Powers be returned immediately. The hospital personnel are forced to comply
even though Powers remains unconscious and untreated.

A day or so later, Powers regains consciousness. He is chained in a spread-eagle
position, hands and feet to a raised concrete slab. He sees there is a guard seated
nearby, writing something down in a green log book. Powers asks what is going on
and is told he is under observation on what is called a "suicide watch." A little
while later, a nurse comes in to take a blood pressure reading, check the bandage,
and ask a lot of questions. Powers tells them that he is not going to live the way
they are trying to force him to live. They all huddle around just outside of Powers'
presence and have a conference.

About a week later Powers is transferred to a mental health medical facility in
Springfield, Missouri, for an evaluation. The doctors there affirm the previous
diagnoses of PTSD and indicate it is likely being made worse by confining Powers
in the ADX control unit. Powers is placed back on his medications and stabilizes.
As soon as the evaluation is completed, Powers is transferred right back to the

ADX control unit. He is taken off of his medication and placed back into the same cell he was in when he rammed his head into the door casing.

PSYCHOLOGIST: Are you still thinking about suicide?

POWERS: Does any of this make any sense to you? Them bringing me right back here, taking me off my medications, and putting me back in the same cell?

PSYCHOLOGY: Well, it does if you think someone might be malingering in order to escape or to get out of doing his control unit time.

POWERS: Is that what you think?

PSYCHOLOGY: No, but there are people who are higher on the totem pole who do think so, and they are the ones who make these kinds of decisions. The report from Springfield is fairly clear about your diagnosis and the fact that your condition is being exacerbated by your assignment to the control unit. The fact is custody always overrides treatment.

POWERS: Thank you for being honest with me. I know what I am going to have to do.

I am trying to write this with my right hand, but it refuses to cooperate. There are no typewriters or word processors at the ADX, so everything I write is in longhand. I stand on the bunk and use the empty TV stand as a desk. But my hand cramps up and will not act right. I have the pen tied with a string to my hand. The only option is to begin writing with my left hand. I have noticed too, that my eyesight is getting bad. In the hallway the other day, I could not make out which guard was standing at the end of the range. My eyes are adjusting to seeing everything up close. I know I have a blazing headache right now and am going to lie down.

> *The kind of pain that causes thoughts of suicide is not physical*
> *pain, but emotional pain. The mind and body are two different*
> *things. The human mind is much more delicate than people*
> *know, and it can be injured in ways that are far more*
> *devastating than physical injury. It seems that the mind*
> *understands it can get relief by getting away from the body. But*
> *the body will not let go of the mind. The biological imperative*

of survival is too strong, too powerful. Feelings of hopelessness
and despair are not usually enough to overcome the body's
need to keep breathing. People live within terrible conditions
because they are unable to die. The mind suffers because the
body holds it in place.

My head hurts all the time. I am pretty sure I fractured my skull when I ran headfirst into the door frame. I am having more of the same thoughts I had before my head was cracked open. It just makes no sense to me! Why is it these so-called officials cannot see that I am seriously trying to be a good person? Is it because once they went to all the trouble of labelling me as a bad person there was no turning back? I cannot understand how or why this nightmare is happening to me. These people are doing horrible things to me under the aegis of public authority, but they have no idea what they are doing!

One thing that is clear to me is that neither judges, prosecutors, or prison officials know how to distinguish between right and wrong. They truly believe they are doing the public a great service by putting bad guys away but everyone who comes through the door with a number is a bad guy! They have no motivation to make such distinctions. Historically, it was the parole board that made such distinctions, but in the federal system the parole board has been abolished for decades. There is no viable mechanism for extending credit where credit is due. So, what is left is a purely punitive agenda that automatically puts all prisoners in the same category.

There is no rational relationship between the sentence imposed and the results of that sentence. Those who have never spent a day locked inside a cage should not be deciding the effect of being locked in a cage. It is like anyone who commits a federal offense has forfeited their lives to the caprice of those who thrive on inflicting punishment as retribution. It is not that much different than ancient rulers who meted out draconian punishments without though or concern. Admittedly, there are some sick, dangerous, and demented individuals who must be kept in prison, but there are others who made mistakes and want to correct them. Many legislators, judges, and prosecutors think that some people mostly people of color are born criminals and that it is a waste of time to try to rehabilitate them.

Probably many people would change if they only knew how to
do it. it is not that easy, though. It is a steep hill to climb with
no obvious reason to even try. How can anyone be aware of his
or her mistakes before they make them? That kind of self-
awareness is not natural to most people. It might be best to

37

*constantly admit that we are all stupid. It is closer to the truth
than thinking we already know it all... it seems that if we think
we are doing it wrong, we may take steps to find out what it
takes to do it right. some mistakes are worse than others, of
course, and maybe some cannot be corrected. Nevertheless, the
essential elements of human compassion and respect cannot be
removed from the equation without foul consequences.*

Every 90 days the Executive Review Panel comes around. Prisoners who are
confined in the control unit have the right to appear before the panel to raise any
issues or concerns they may have and to review their progress. Hardly any
prisoners even attend. The guard came around this morning and asked if I wanted
to go out there this afternoon, and I said I would. It is usually the director, the
Warden, the associate Wardens, the captain, and the case manager who are in
attendance.

DIRECTOR: Mr. Powers, this is the Executive Committee Review Panel.
We have reviewed your packet and have determined to continue you in the
control unit. Due to your misconduct, you have not received credit for the
past month. Do you have any questions?

POWERS: Yeah, I have a question. Why is there no curriculum on how to
become a better human being by way of character building?

DIRECTOR: (looking at Warden) We have some educational materials
available to them, don't we?

WARDEN: He is not going to be able to receive them because he is on a TV
restriction. The education department plays them on the institutional
channels from time to time.

POWERS: That's not what I'm talking about. I'm talking about some kind of
a course that prisoners could take that would help them to become better
human beings by improving their personal character.

DIRECTOR: Well, we are doing all we can with the resources that are
available. Anything else? All right--
POWERS: It just seems like something more could be done to help the men
who are here rather than to keep driving them down. Can't we get some kind
of work or have productive activities?

DIRECTOR: (to Warden) What's the status on him getting a TV?

WARDEN: He has a lot of disciplinary segregation time left.

DIRECTOR: We can look at it another time, then. (To Powers) Keep programming and stay out of trouble and we will see you again the next time…

POWERS: … But there is no programming. That is what I am trying to tell you.

WARDEN: If you want to file a formal complaint you can get a BP-9 form from the counselor. That will be all, Powers.

They want me to feel small and helpless, and maybe I am small and helpless. I want to fight back, but the system they have here is a monster. It seems as though they want me to sit in the middle of the floor and twiddle my thumbs all day long. There is not much I can do. To file grievances is a waste of time because the people who are being complained about are the very ones who are answering the complaint. Of course they are going to deny whatever I have to say or suggest. I already tried to write to a couple of senators and to the editor of the Denver Post, but those letters probably had as much chance to make it past the gates as I do.

The door clanked shut in the cell beneath mine. This means that they just put someone in that cell. It is a special security cell that has Plexiglass on the inner bars so a prisoner cannot throw anything on or at the guards. I heard chains being dragged around, so this means whoever is in that cell is in what are called "ambulatory restraints." It is shackles, handcuffs, and a belly chain. It is a pain in the ass too because you have to sleep in them, walk in them, shower in them, take a dump in them, and everything else. The guards come around every 2 hours to check the restraints. It is no good.

> The chains are around my ankles, around my waist, and around
> my wrists. I am shuffling up the ramp at the transfer center.
> There are a couple of hundred other prisoners who are equally
> chained. It is hard to even breathe with the shit around my belly
> so tight, and my hands have been numb for hours...I sit down on
> a long wooden bench and wait to get processed. There are quite
> a few female prisoners who are up ahead, waiting to have their

chains removed. I am sickened and appalled by the sight of all these women in chains. There is even a pregnant woman who is in chains handcuffs, belly chain, shackles the whole works! It is terrible. It hits me like an ice-cold knife in the middle of my chest and sinks in deep: this sudden understanding. They use these diabolical devices in an attempt to break your spirit and to inflict physical pain. It is not security, for what are those hapless women going to do? It is an insidious design, one that harkens back to the inquisitions and dungeons of old.

The Concept of Time

IN prison, the concept of time is different than it is on the outside. Contrary to popular belief, there are not many prisoners who keep calendars. It may seem like a month is a long time, but when a person is counting the days, a month might seem like a year. Mostly, prisoners gauge their time in other ways. The routines of prison life are like a clock, and prisoners mark time by events. For them, time is the perception of change. If there is nothing much that changes, time remains regular and uneventful. As a prisoner, you can stay on the top side of time by ignoring it; or you can be underneath its weight by giving it too much attention and credibility. This means that you do not worry about a release date or put your life on hold until your sentence is up. You adjust to your circumstances, keep on living your life, and stop judging things by the measure of time.

As time goes by in our lives, everyone feels that something is being lost by being left behind. And there is a certain sadness that lingers like the smell of something that has died. We try to avoid this feeling, but it tends to stay with us and may even overcome us. the real question is not how long we have left to do or to be, but where is time taking us? does time itself have an end? Is death some terrible and unacceptable result of time? I have already been dead several times, and I can tell you how it goes: your body knows that death is imminent, and it begins to shut down. You feel a bit panicked because a very dark sensation sweeps over your entire being. It is powerful and intense, but it only lasts a moment or so before it goes away. Then, a peaceful and calm feeling begins to flood your body and mind; and you feel no further pain, or fear, or regret. At about that point, you lose consciousness. Now, my heart did not actually stop all the way, so I did not have an out of body experience or see any light. I recall nothing except nothingness. The real question of time is this: can you accept no longer existing?

Powers looks at himself in the mirror and is shocked at how he has aged in this place in such a short time. His eyes are not as bright and young as they once were; they appear dull and have lost their sense of hope. There is anger hiding behind them...The time lies heavy upon his mind, pressing inward and trying to squeeze it like a vise. There is a certain desperation and despair involved a heaviness on the soul that pushes downward with a sure and steady strength. Any resistance produces an internal grind that smells like the acrid, stagnant air of a crypt. It is an intolerable situation because Powers keeps on losing ground. He wonders how the other prisoners are able to be all right with it.

The prisoner in the cell below me is called Gato. He is a young Puerto Rican kid from New York City who has some serious mental issues going on. I have been talking with him via the sink drain. Evidently, he has an assload of time on some drug conspiracy case. He assaulted an associate Warden at USP Lewisburg, Pennsylvania and got an assload of more time and was sent over here to the control unit. He too has been to USP Springfield and back. They did about the same thing said he needed to be on meds and needed treatment outside of the control unit. So much for that.

Yesterday he asked me if I had heard the guards come into his cell the night before. He claims they attacked him sometime after midnight, and he insists that they drugged him and raped him. I told him I had not heard anything because I was sleeping. I also told him that I did not think the guards would go that that length, and this made him mad at me. I do know they have been doing bogus shit to him. Apparently, the guards and administrators have no love for either one of us. But I like Gato. He seems to be a good-hearted kid who got caught up in much more than what he ever dreamed possible.

GATO: They keep throwing my food on the floor in the sally port.

POWERS: They're still giving you a bag lunch?

GATO: Yeah, bologna sandwich but they open the bag and dump it into the sally port. I have to fish it out of there and wash it off because they are poisoning my food.

POWERS: They are poisoning the bologna?

GATO: That and the bread and the fruit, too. It tastes like chemicals and knocks me out. That's when they come in and assault me.

POWERS: I think I would have heard the doors opening, but I didn't hear anything. Could you have been having a bad dream?

GATO: This was no dream, man! This has happened many times. They know what they are doing to me. This is why they keep me in chains all the time so I can't fight back!

POWERS: And they sexually assault you?

GATO: Look, they have been doing this to me for a long time.… Hold up a minute. I think I hear someone on the range. I'll get back with you later.

Anything around Powers' neck makes him panic and resist. He has already experimented. The trouble is that he does not want his loved ones to think poorly about him. He has some strange idea that he can give himself an infection that will kill him. He rubs dirt and grime into the burns on his legs and torso but cannot get the infection to take. About a week ago, he ate ten tubes of toothpaste and swallowed half a bottle of aspirin. It nearly killed him, too. He lay in a stupor on the floor for several days with a terrible belly ache and his ears ringing. Almost all of his hair fell out. It was a terrible experience that he vowed not to try again.

We are at a funeral for an old woman. My grandpa knew her, but we never did. She is wearing a button-down sweater, white with blue buttons. Her hair is done up nicely and her hands are folded peacefully across her waist. Her eyes are closed but she is wearing her glasses. There are pictures of her when she was alive that are propped up near the casket. Several older women are in the front row and are crying. I am standing there looking at the body that has no life left in it. Was there a soul that once inhabited this flesh, I wonder. if so, where has it gone? I want to reach for her hand, but I already know it is hard and cold and dead. It seems a mystery to me.

Death has become a bit of an obsession. I think about it all the time. I toy with it because I no longer have any respect for it. It seems I am trying to get used to the idea of being dead. I think about the billions of human beings who have already lived their lives on Earth and are now, literally, dust in the wind. It occurs to me that I do not like being human; it is too strange and too difficult. Whether I continue to exist or not is not much of a concern to me. I find myself going along with the general scheme of things, but I feel I am only biding my time. The edge of time is sharp, and it is stained with the blood of everyone it has taken into the void.

The one thing I do not want is for death to come to me, for I would rather go to it. I want to meet it head on and force its hand. Otherwise, I feel like I am dodging and ducking something I must face in any event at some point in time, and I hate that feeling. It is coming. I can feel its presence all around me. It is with me all of the time now, and it seems to be more of a friend than an enemy. I am biding my time, riding the wave, and waiting for the end of this reality.

POWERS: You feel like playing some chess?

GATO: They won't give me a board.

POWERS: No, we can make them ourselves.

GATO: I don't have anything to make one out of.

POWERS: I will make one for you and slide it down the crack in the back wall.

GATO: Okay! Make the pieces, too.

POWERS: I will put letters across the top and numbers down the left side. That will make it easy to call the moves.

GATO: We will both have a board, right?

POWERS: Yeah. And we will both have pieces. That way, we both have each other's pieces and a board.

GATO: But you know I'm the Chess Master, right?

POWERS: We'll find out soon enough.

GATO: Let's play for push-ups.

POWERS: You can't do push-ups in those chains!

GATO: I'm not the one who's going to be doing them

The Suicide Cells

THERE is a phase of training for guards that is called annual training. They go to the gun range, attend classes, listen to lectures by administrative staff, get out of work early, and hit the nearest bars. Mostly everyone involved goes through the motions without taking it too seriously. To be fair, though the Federal Bureau of Prisons does its best to maintain a high level of training in a professional atmosphere. The problem is always the individuals who think they already know it all or who have enough seniority to not give a damn. It is all part of an extensive dog and pony show anyway.

There are always a few guards who know they cannot be readily fired or sanctioned, and they are usually the ones who do their best to convey punishment to the prisoners. They sometimes take it upon themselves to inflict punishments that they themselves make up. For example, they write false incident reports in order to get privileges and good time credits taken away. They can intentionally withhold mail, food, laundry, hygiene items, recreation periods, telephone calls, et cetera. They can berate the prisoner, make sexual comments, or pass around false and malicious information about one prisoner to another. They can set a prisoner up by claiming they found contraband in his cell. They can tamper with the food trays or intimate that they tampered with the food trays. They can manhandle a prisoner and claim he was failing to follow their orders or was otherwise resisting.

I am tired of these guards harassing me. They have been banging the outer door with their sticks while I am trying to read or write, and it is like a rifle shot inside the cell. They jacked my legal papers the other day while I was recreation, and they have me on the drug test sheet. It is like an everyday thing, and I am getting fed up with it. I am not trying to be made sport of by these morons, yet there is not much I can do about it either. They do not know how close I am to checking out of this dump. If there was a button on the wall I could push that would blow up this entire prison, I would not even hesitate. I am ready to go.

Powers is on the table in one of the examination rooms in the prison infirmary, and he is bleeding profusely. The doctor, an older gentleman who is actually a good doctor, is trying to stop the bleed. Powers is semiconscious and is moving his head from side to side and moaning. The blood is thick and dark. Then powers tries to raise up, two guards move in to hold him down. The chains are still binding his legs and wrists and will not be removed under any circumstances. The doctor instructs the

*nurse to start an I.V. line and places an oxygen mask over
Powers' face. Powers falls unconscious and, when he next
awakens, he is in a hospital room being transfused with blood.
He falls back into sleep.*

It is freezing cold in the cell. Powers is lying on a mattress that is on top of a
concrete slab. The deep indentations from the handcuffs and leg irons are pressed
into the flesh of his ankles and wrists. He is wearing a green smock that is held in
place with Velcro straps. His hands are swelled, and he moves his fingers to see if
they still work. There is a guard who is stationed just outside the door. He is on
overtime pay and has a newspaper in his hands, perusing the sports section. There
is no sink or toilet in the cell.

    POWERS: Can I read the paper when you are done?

    GUARD: Can't do it. You can't have anything in there you might hurt
    yourself with.

    POWERS: How can I hurt myself with a newspaper?

    GUARD: No newspaper, Powers.

    POWERS: Are you even supposed to be reading it? I thought your job was
    to watch me to make sure I am not killing myself.

    GUARD: Do you still feel suicidal?

    POWERS: I am still in prison, aren't I? I will probably be suicidal for the
    duration.

    GUARD: The doctors will be by in a bit, and you can talk to them. If you are
    still suicidal, they will probably keep you on watch.

    POWERS: A cage is a cage is a cage…

Most of the psychologists have no idea about how to provide helpful treatment to
prisoners. They consider prisoners to be malingering. If they are pressed to supply
a diagnosis, they diagnose prisoners as having antisocial personality disorder,
which is not a good diagnosis to have. The very idea of treatment is antithetical to
the stated purposes of the federal supermax's control unit. That is why prisoners

who have serious mental disorders are not supposed to be placed there. One of the most pointed problems is that the psychologists are not really psychologists: they are, first and foremost, correctional officers.

This is not to say that some prison psychologists are not their own persons. There are a few who truly do want to help, but once they are found out by the administration, they are run off. In some ways, the psychologists have a lot of power. A lot of prisoners will not even talk to a prison psychologist for fear of what they can do with their reports. They can easily become malicious and misuse their power to make life even more miserable for prisoners particularly those they happen to dislike. For example, they can order forced medication, changed cell assignments, restrictions on personal property, and even commitments. They can have a prisoner kept pretty much naked inside a cold cell for as long as they want to.

There is one psychologist who works here who does her best to help people. I keep thinking, hey, wait a minute, I am an American citizen, but that status is not recognized here. They want to make me jump through hoops. If the role were reversed, those who get angry at me for speaking my mind would likely be doing the same. The prisoncrats act like I am some foreign enemy because I complain about the lack of adequate mental health care. They act like I have done something wrong when I insist on being treated like a human being. This one psychologist is not afraid to go against the grain. She appears to be a real human being, which is rare and constitutes a breath of fresh air to me. She probably will not last long in this environment.

> POWERS: So I ask myself, what am I doing here? I lose track of time. It seems like hours should have passed but it is only a few minutes. Why can't it be the other way around? I don't care about the person I always thought of as being me; I no longer want to be him.
>
> PSYCHOLOGIST: Are you saying you lose touch with reality sometimes?
>
> POWERS: No, I think I'm too much in touch with reality. (shrugs) What can be done? This is now what I am left with. It isn't much.
>
> PSYCHOLOGIST: I agree. The control unit policy is being misused. There are quite a few of you guys who have been diagnosed with a mental illness, but you are stuck there without treatment. I understand where you are coming from.

POWERS: What can be done? I'm stuck with an intolerable situation.

PSYCHOLOGIST: Well, I can come down and meet with you once or twice a month. I can bring you some books from our department that you might find interesting. We do have a workbook for PTSD that I can bring.

POWERS: That would be great.

During the few times when I feel less stressed or less hopeless, I think that correctional officers and other staff are not some kind of knuckle-dragging thugs. They are an assortment of human being who have the same kind of feelings and stressors that other people do. The majority of them probably want to do the right thing, but they are trapped in a role. Prison policies change all the time, so they never quite have anything solid to go by. They have to be around a bunch of thieves, rapists, murderers and morons all day long. They have to put up with a good deal of BS coming from the top down. They go through hard times themselves. It is not an easy lift for them either.

It is a hot summer day. Luckily, the city park is very close by, and it boasts a nice swimming pool. It is one of the rare occasions when the entire family is going to the park for swimming and picnicking. There is a lawnmower repair shop adjacent to the park, and I have been going there regularly. There is an old black man named Lee who works there. He sometimes opens the soda machine to get me a cold coca cola. On this day I ask lee if he can give me enough coca-colas for my family. He readily agrees. He opens the machine and is loading bottles into my arms when his boss pulls up. The boss makes us put the sodas back into the machine. I am waiting by the door while Lee and his boss begin to argue about the sodas. I hear Lee's boss tell him to pick up his tools and to get out that he is fired... I wait for lee to come out so I can apologies for getting him into trouble. he puts his tools inside his little beat-up old car and tells me not to worry about it. the boss comes out and locks the door behind him. he stares at me, and I begin to walk toward the park with my head down. I am confused and ashamed, and I am sorry for old man Lee.

They finally take me back to my cell in the control unit. Gato is like a long-lost friend; he wants to know what happened in detail, and I have nothing but time. He tells me that he will never commit suicide. He says that he wants to hang around and give them hell until he dies at a ripe old age. On the other side of my mind I know that I am still on borrowed time free time, if put another way. I am physically weakened and need to sleep a lot. I perform my yoga asanas on shaky limbs and find myself hungry for meat. It takes me a good three months to recover enough to keep up with Gato's exercise routine. He is young enough to be my son, and I am sympathetic toward him.

We are both going through a lot. The guards mess with me a little, but they mess with Gato a lot. I can often hear them down there, standing in his sally port, yelling at him. He yells right back at them, too. He has told me about some of the stuff they have done to him. One time he barricaded himself with a mattress inside the shower and they had to suit up and come in on him. Once they had him down on the floor, they sprayed CS gas up his ass. He said that he had never felt such burning pain before and that all he could do was weep like a small child. It broke my heart to hear it, but I had already heard and seen plenty a lot of it up close and personal. Some of we prisoners were in a life and death struggle every day while the others kicked back eating potato chips, watching TV and jacking off.

> *Ultimately each prisoner has to decide how he is going to do his time. Those who decide to act out for whatever reason have to be willing to accept the consequences. Certain prisoners understand right away that there is no win in bucking the system, and they lay down and fall back. They do not necessarily mind if other prisoners raise hell, and sometimes they even encourage them to do so. Other prisoners get angry at any other prisoner who causes a disturbance, or, for that matter, who do anything out of the ordinary. Many of the prisoners who are housed at the ADX have killed a prisoner elsewhere for the very purpose of getting to the ADX. This is an ongoing phenomenon in the Federal Penitentiary system. They figure they can at least have their own cells, a TV set, and some peace and quiet. They actually like doing their time at the ADX. They feel they have worked their way to the top.*

Losing a Finger

THE guard come down the range with the food cart at the same time every afternoon. They key the heavy food slot doors and let them drop open of their own weight. It makes loud gunshot like noise. The inner cell door all steel bars opens with a loud clank, and the guard flops a set of trays down on the food slot. The food is healthy but not very tasty. Mostly it is beans and rice and some additional vegetable. A prisoner down the range is hollering about something missing from his tray probably an attempt to get something extra. A moment ago it was so quiet you could hear a pin drop, and now it seems noisy. I have asked the guards to stop dropping the food slot doors, but they have completely ignored the request. The problem is that it triggers a startle response that floods my entire body with adrenaline instantly, and it makes me ready for combat!

I am deep into my writing when the food slot drops open with a bang. It startles me and I drop my pen on the floor. For some reason I am especially pissed off about it. I jump down and grab the food trays, and the guard slams the slot. I set the trays down and put my little finger across the steel door casing where the electronically controlled inner cell door will slam closed. the door whines and cuts across its tracks. I hold my finger right there and the door slams closed on it. The steel edges on the door and frame have nearly severed it. There is a lot of blood! I never knew the little finger had an artery in it, but it sure does! The guard has to get control to open the inner door again so I can get my finger out. It hurts like holy hell, is spurting blood, and is hanging by a thin piece of skin. The guard demands to know why I did it, and I tell him I did it because he keeps slamming my food slot.

As of late, Powers has been putting up with a lot of frustration, torment and stress. He has not been allowed to make phone calls to respond to family matters, his commissary account is frozen, and he is the prime target of other prisoners and staff. The asshole in the next cell over keeps pounding on the wall between them at all times of the day and night. Just when Powers thinks the dude has stopped BAM! BAM! BAM! there he goes again. The prisoner on the other side has been kicking his shower, and that sounds like a big bass drum. The orderly has taken to emptying the mop bucket under Powers' door. It is rare for Powers to get more than an hour's sleep at a time, and he is having a lot of headaches.

The partially severed finger is reattached. The administration had to arrange an outside trip to a specialist. It is an eventful field trip. I was able to see the countryside and cars and people. The security they employ, however, was like something out of a Hollywood film set like a S.W.A.T. operation. The guards wore all black protective gear, carried MP5 submachine guns, and maintained ongoing radio contact. They kept me all chained up in the back of an unmarked prison van with a stun belt on my leg. Two chase cars kept switching positions as we sped down the road. The driver cranked up the volume on rock station
so that I could not hear what he and his comrade in the passenger seat were talking about. They were all having fun.

They were having fun until they saw where the surgeon had his office: it was in a modified home near a public park. The nurses made the guards put on some type of surgical suits and matching hats that made them look like bunny rabbits. It was a lot of everything for one little finger. The doctor's staff must have thought I was some big time mafioso or a mass murderer or something. I remember them putting on some music in the operating room and me joking about the bunny rabbits coming out of the closet. The next thing I knew, I was back in the van and racing back to the prison complex.

GATO: Did they put your finger back on?

POWERS: Yeah, they put a steel pin through the bone, and it is still sticking out the tip of my
finger.

GATO: Didn't that hurt like hell when you did that?

POWERS: Not really. I was in some kind of a weird state of mind. I just didn't care.

GATO: Man, you took on the B.O.P. with your little finger! I'll bet it cost them a lot of money, too.

POWERS: Yeah, but I don't think they care about any of that, either.

GATO: Do you smell anything coming through the vents?

POWERS: No, why?

GATO: Because they've been putting some kind of chemical agent in my vent again. It has a strong chemical odor. You don't smell it up there?

POWERS: No.

GATO: You wouldn't believe what they've been doing to me since you left for your finger. I've already filed complaints with the courts, but they isn't doing jack shit about it.

POWERS: Well, how about a game of chess? Take our minds off of the bullshit for a few minutes.

GATO: Yeah, okay. Sounds good. Give me a minute.

People may think that the federal courts are responsive to the complaints of prisoners who are being subjected to unconstitutional conditions of confinement, but they would be wrong. The courts typically take a "hands off" approach and allow prison officials to operate their prisons without legal supervision. The way the law is set up makes it nearly impossible for prisoners to get relief. Plus, the courts are heavily prejudiced against prisoners in the first place. For every complaint that makes it to a court there might be a thousand violations that went unreported.

Anyone who brings a complaint must follow a labyrinth of rules and time limits in order to even get a foot in the door. The prison officials have a few tricks up their sleeves to make it next to impossible. In effect, the prisoner has to go up against layer after layer of governmental machinery designed to do away with their complaints. At best it is some dude in a stark prison cell writing legal documents on notebook paper in longhand and going up against professionals whose entire career goals are centered on the nuances of the law. It is anything but a level playing field. The vast majority of prisoners are wasting their time.

I continue with my studies and writing. All of my writing is now left-handed block printing on lined prison-issued paper. In high school I liked English, but my grades were not that good. But when I came to prison I began to study composition, and I read a lot of books by the masters. Of course, I also wrote a ton of letters. There is nothing I like better than to be up at night, standing on the concrete bunk, and using the TV shelf on the wall by the light to write on. It provides me with a way to express myself, and it supplies me with a refuge. When I am writing, I am no longer inside of a cage.

Writing makes me feel like I am accomplishing something. It allows me to believe that my life has some kind of purpose beyond life in a cage. I envy the great authors, their words, and the way they arrange them. It is like constructing a building with words instead of with bricks. When I begin to run short on materials, I pace back and forth and keep my mind open for parts and pieces and designs I can use. There are so many human beings who have such remarkable stories, and so many of them will never be told.....

Sometimes I find myself thinking out loud, that is, talking to myself. And then there are times when a groundswell of emotion sweeps over me, and I begin to cry for no discernable reason. I think that something must be happening to one of my loved ones on the outside and that I am picking up those vibrations. I am so utterly broken hearted. At these times I have to get into the shower and squat down and let the water run over me while I cry out the pain. It is at times like these that I feel hopeless, helpless, and alone. I have people who I love but am separated from by unrelenting circumstances. It is not a good feeling.

> *The emptiness of life can destroy the spirit. It is very hard to keep it alive when it is starving for expression but has no expression available. The starving, dying spirit wreathes in pain as it suffers the vagaries of the flesh. All it wants is to be free from the constant constraints. To the spirit, the extinction of the flesh is liberty, and this drive is in everyone. The mind that is controlled by the flesh keeps vying for physical survival at any and all costs. But the mind that is controlled by the spirit keeps on trying to find a way out. They are opposed in their goals, and this conflict is natural to all human beings. There is something in our design that results in this well-known dualism and conflict.*

Gato keeps telling me about how beautiful Puerto Rico is when the sun is setting on the horizon of the ocean. He still has family there that he talks about frequently. There is not much difference between how he feels and how I feel. Yeah, we both committed criminal offenses that resulted in lengthy prison sentences; yeah, we both committed misconduct while in prison that ended us up at the ADX supermax; yeah, we were both sent to the control unit where we could not readily adapt. And now we are both trying to figure out which way to go and what to do, and we are confused and angry and lost. There is not much we can do to change what has happened, what we have done, what has been done to us.

53

Good Days, Bad Days

THERE are good days and there are bad days. In some ways they compete with one another. I can usually tell when it is going to be a bad day because there is a feeling in the air. In addition, something will occur that throws everything off or turns things negative. The good days are good days by default; that is, when it is not a bad day it is a good day. And it is always the little things that make for a good day: a decent meal, a piece of mail, or a cup of coffee. It does not take much. But then, it does not take much to make it a bad day, either.

Sometimes it may be that my perspective is pointed either one way or the other at the beginning of the day. One small offset is usually not enough to make a good day a bad day, or vice versa. Those who live their lives inside cages are looking for a little relief from the monotony; they want to feel good for a little while. But the administration does not allow it if and when it can prevent it. This is why whenever a prisoner does find some means of breaking through the boredom to feel like a real human being for a time, the fun busters will show up to knock it all down. My good days are mostly during the night when I have a candle burning and am seated on my blanket, meditating and thinking.

PSYCHOLOGIST: Hello, Mr. Powers. I was making rounds and thought I'd stop by. How are you doing?

POWERS: I am doing all right.

PSYCHOLOGIST: How is that finger healing up?

POWERS: It seems to be coming along just fine. I think they take the pin out next week.

PSYCHOLOGIST: (puts papers on the bars) I brought you a copy of our book list. If you see anything you'd like to read, send me a cop-out.

POWERS: Oh, thanks...The chaplains have been bringing me some good stuff from their library, but I can always learn more.

PSYCHOLOGIST: What are you working on now?

POWERS: Studying early Christianity and ancient culture. Egyptian, Mesopotamian, and Persian mostly. It is quite interesting.

PSYCHOLOGIST: Well, I would like to come back on Monday and pull you out so we can talk more.

POWERS: Sure. That sounds good.

This new psychologist seems to be a relatively decent human being. I do not know what she can do for me, if anything. The only thing I can think of is to move me out of the control unit, put me back on the proper medications, and set up some kind of a comprehensive treatment plan. But none of this is likely to happen no matter what she says or does. The dictates of custody overrule the premises of effective treatment every time. In the meantime, it is good that she wants to have me pulled out so we can converse in
relative privacy. The other prisoners will definitely be jealous about that.

> *We are on a fishing trip on the St. Lawrence seaway in upstate New York. It has been a long, hot day. We have been on the water for many hours now and it is starting to get dark. It is finally time to head on back to the campsite. for the last hour or so I have been using a worm, hook, and sinker and have left my line in the water while everyone else is still casting. As soon as I begin to reel in my line, something hits it. At first I think it has snagged a sunken log or something, but whatever it is begins to move out into the deeper river. I set the drag, and the fish takes a lot of line. I struggle with this monster for a long time, losing line and then gaining line. The fish or whatever it was breaks the surface about fifty yards out and then dives. My line spins all the way out and breaks off. We all look at each other and speculate about what it could have been. I am somewhat disappointed, but I still feel lucky to have hooked into it in the first place.*

Who am I fooling? This planet sucks! There is nothing of any consequence going on here. We do not even know where we came from or how we came to be humans. Look at an insect and think about how bizarre it is, how alien it looks. There is something wrong with this picture. We human beings make no sense; we are an anomaly! We have been tricked, shit on, abandoned. Whatever sick and demented creatures made human beings did a shoddy job of it. The least they could have done is to give us some sense. All we have to hang on to is the concept of

"God" a concept that has caused more murder and mayhem among humans that anything else ever could. It is embarrassing!

I am nothing, nothing at all. I keep on trying to think that I am something, but my life has no importance whatsoever. I only exist due to happenstance. It is all animal instincts. The fact that we have the ability to talk, opposable thumbs, and a creative intellect is simply cruelty. Human beings are one big disaster in the making! Yes, I am mad about it, too. It is sad to think that one set of dangerous animals is able to keep another set of dangerous animals in cages they call prisons. I am not wrong about this. "Eat, drink and be merry," is the best advice for a race of beings that are so misguided and ignorant….

When I was at another prison, I used to sell homemade wine. I had a 5-gallon bucket with a lid that I kept under the bunk in a green Army issued duffel bag. I would put 1 gallon of tomato puree (liberated from food service), 8 pounds of sugar (liberated from service), 3 gallons of water, and a pinch of yeast and mix it. I kept it ventilated at the top with a tube that went inside a bottle of baby powder. The yeast feeds on the sugar and multiplies quickly. At first there is an abundance of sugar, and the yeast gobbles up everything in sight. But then the yeast begin to fight over the remaining sugar. They poop alcohol and begin to die off. Little by little they all die off and leave behind a fair percentage of alcohol.

Powers thinks about all the times gone by and relives them in his mind. All of the memories of youthful adventure come back to him, and he gets to experience them again. It is like some other person who was there in those times and did those things. It is like watching a movie. Powers went to prison at the ripe old age of twenty-seven. He does not accept his life within the cage, so he tries to avoid it as much as possible. In a way, he does feel sorry for himself, but only because of the abuses perpetrated on him by government officials. He feels that no official can be authorized to demonize and torture another. Moreover, he thinks he is seriously misunderstood.

> *It seems nearly impossible to find myself in the way I need to be found. Everything here is so upside down that I find it confusing. Do those in positions of authority want me to reform my basic personal character or do they want me to become worse? Is this extensive and harsh punishment for purposes of retribution or correction? It cannot be for both at the same time because they are mutually exclusive in their applications. Punishment for the purposes of inflicting harms cannot be*

*justified under a scheme of corrections because it does not help
and is only intended to hurt. Putting demeaning labels on
people does not help to correct aberrant behavior. Why is it
that the authorities resist the kinds of instruction and
motivational influences that would equip a person for life as a
decent human being?*

It is true that I remain at a loss for how any of this madness can be proper within
the scope of valid penological goals that are based on societal standards of law and
order. I complain about it a lot because it seems so wrong to me that I must. But
my small and pathetic voice cannot be heard above the din of the machinery. A lot
of people are hiding behind the curtains and pulling levers that, in effect, crush
people and burn them up in this incinerator, and profit from the process by
charging for the service. We desperately require a new and improved criminal
justice system, but there is no way it will ever happen.

Nobody Hearing Me

WHO else is there to reach out to? I have written to senators, congressmen, lawyers, judges, private organizations, and newspapers. Most of the time I do not receive an answer. I have also filed numerous requests for administrative remedy. I have to be on point and watch for the counselor to go past in order to get the forms from him. He tries to slide on past quickly, and he will not come back if I miss him. He is in a hurry because he leaves a few hours early every day. I figure that he has robbed the taxpayers for far more money than I ever got from a bank.

There are very few checks on federal employees especially at the ADX where certain staff members can leave for lunch and not return until the next day. There are all kinds of crimes and infractions they commit and get away with. They steal government property, they falsify official documents and records, they violate rules and regulations. They have nearly complete immunity. People who are on the outside of the prison industrial complex do not have a means of doing anything. Elected officials do not want to waste their time on prisoners because there is nothing in it for them. Private organizations are too busy and too underfunded to do very much. It is a steep hill to climb.

> *During the fifteenth and sixteenth centuries in Europe an institutionalized phenomena that reared its ugly head throughout European nations. it was based on ignorance, fear, and superstition. Men, women, and children were pulled out of their homes, tied up with restraints, and taken to the local jails. there, they were accused of being demons or witches or the offspring of such. The authorities proceeded to torture them with some of the most insidious devices known to mankind. They were burned and bent and cut and stabbed and squeezed and torn in order to extract confessions. The so-called authorities were convinced of their own righteousness, but what really mattered to them was the fact that they were in control. This inquisitional hysteria turned into an economic power-house for the perpetrators. People were terrified to speak out against any of it for fear they themselves would be subjected to it. Tens of thousands of good and decent human beings were hideously murdered by those who called themselves good people. The enormity of their deeds eventually caught up with them as they became more and more aware of their own guilt.*

There are not all that many ways to protest inhumane living conditions, unfair sentences, or wrongful acts by prison officials. The grievances against prison officials are heard and responded to by the same prison officials. If a prison is able to file a civil rights complaint, the courts are quick to throw it out. Some prisoners will go on a hunger strike, but these are hard to organize and even harder to maintain.

Prison staff knows exactly how to defeat hunger strikes. They isolate the prisoner after a few days, remove all food items from his cell, and begin a watch protocol. They will even go so far as to shut off the tap water in the cell to make sure the prisoner cannot fill his belly with water. After a determined time, guards will offer the prisoner a tasty looking meal. They never give in to any of the prisoner's demands or requests; and if enough time goes by, they will begin force feeding the prisoner. They use a rigid feeding tube that they shove through the nose and down the throat while the prisoner is chained down.

Occasionally, prisoners will barricade themselves inside the cell. They typically use the mattress as a shield, cover the windows or the bars at the front of the cells, begin to break things, and trigger the sprinkler inside the cell. The response by prison staff is all too routine: they suit up a "team," go to the cell front, shoot a cannister or two of CS gas into the cell, and then rush inside and tackle the prisoner. If the prisoner has a weapon or is barricaded in a way that guards cannot see whether he has a weapon, they will shoot non-lethal projectiles to disable him. If need be, they will use percussion grenades to stun the prisoner before they enter the cell.

Some prisoners will flood the range or set fires. The fires are more dangerous because of the smoke, and they tend to set off a series of piercing alarms. The guards come with fire extinguishers and spray the shit out of the prisoner, his property, and whatever the prisoner has set on fire. Tie prisoner, of course, is lugged off to the hole or chained down to a concrete slab. If there is cleaning up to be done, it is
done by a range orderly. If the orderly on the range where the mess is refuses to do it, they will go get a different orderly from another range to do it. It is rare to see guards cleaning up a prisoner's mess.

To me, the only effective means of protest involve self-harm and suicide. Self-mutilation requires the prison staff to fill out a lot of paperwork, to get the medical staff involved, and to notify the higher-ups. The only problem is, there are not many prisoners who are willing or able to go to these extremes. Some prisoners fake suicide attempts by tying a sheet around the neck and waiting for a guard to come around before making it look like they are hanging. Other prisoners fake overdoses of aspirin and other medications by emptying the capsules or by making fake pills that they swallow in front of a staff member. Cuts to the arms are the usual go-to for those who engage in acts of self-harm, and this is because it is easy and does not hurt much.

But there are also prisoners who are not faking anything. They will continue to attempt suicide until they are successful. The most common form of suicide, by far, is by hanging. The prisoner simply makes a noose or otherwise ties a strip of sheet around his neck and uses his body weight to apply pressure until he passes out. Although the administration may have suicide prevention policies in place, there is no way to stop someone who is truly intent on doing it. Once the circulation to the brain is impeded, it takes only a few minutes to become brain dead. So resuscitation might be successful in terms of getting the prisoner to breathe again, but he is brain dead. They take him to a local hospital and let him die there. Very few prisoners are listed as dying inside the prison. Sometimes prisoners will engage in parasuicide a type of self-harm that can result in death whether intentional or not. Some prisoners swallow sharp objects like pencils, sporks, pieces of metal, or wires. Others shove objects up their penises or up their rectums. There are also those who have a fixation on cutting open their own bellies or sticking sharpened objects into their abdominal cavities. These are typically prisoners who have an underlying mental disorder that is being exacerbated by the conditions of their confinement. A large number of prisoners have PTSD, major depression, or sexual disorders that are undiagnosed and, hence, untreated. Many prisoncrats feel it is a waste of time to treat them.

GATO: Man, Powers, I don't know how much longer I can take this shit.

POWERS: What's up with you?

GATO: You know. They are doing everything they can to fuck with me. How am I supposed to act when they are spraying gas and poison into the vents, tamper with my food, throw my mail in the trash, and come in here at night to assault me and rape me?

POWERS: I don't know, bro. I don't even know what's real anymore. All I can say is that is a bad situation to be in, and I hope we get some help from someplace.

GATO: I am so strung out I don't know what to do.

POWERS: Maybe things will change, but I don't think so.

GATO: No one understands what I am dealing with, Powers. It is terrible! I miss my family so much! They would be better off if I kill myself.

POWERS: Look, maybe something good will happen. Why don't we play a game or two or do a workout get our minds going in another direction?

GATO: All right. But give me a minute or two.

Gato and I are like two peas in a pod. We have a workout that involves a lot of burpees, a lot of squats, and a lot of sit-ups. Sometimes I think that Gato is only pretending to be doing the workout. This is because when I call him he always sounds like he is eating something. I have only seen him one time, and that was from a good distance. He looked to be slightly overweight at that time. But he claims he can do three-hundred and fifty pushups nonstop, and I do not believe it but have no way to know for sure. A lot of what he tells me is pretty far away from what is believable. Nevertheless, I have no reason to burst his bubble by challenging it.

There is no doubt whatsoever in my mind that Gato has some type of a psychosis going on, probably schizophrenia. He is, by far, worse off than I am. There is no one going into his cell to beat him up and rape him every night, but he believes it. I have written to the executive staff and to psychology about him, but I never do get any reply. His situation does not look good to me, but what do I know. This is all outside of anything I can do. It is hard to think about the kind of deliberate indifference that is being demonstrated by staff. The only result I can come up with is that nobody cares, and I do not think this is the way it is supposed to be. It is frustrating for me because I am also worried about him.

The panic attacks come out of nowhere. There is no forewarning or sign or any kind. Everything seems to shift in a way that changes my perception of time and space. My vision gets weird, and it is hard for me to breathe. My heart races like crazy; my skin on my palms and forehead. There is a dizziness but not enough to cause nausea, and I have to either sit or lie down immediately. These episodes began about a year after Eddie was killed and have continued at odd intervals. It seems

there is something going on in the unconscious part of the mind
that is having an effect on the conscious mind and, from there,
the body. this is very much a real thing that is going on, and it
is the result of the PTSD. It is a strange injury because it affects
the psyche in a way that triggers a death instinct turns cold and
clammy; and I break out in a sweat.

There are certain triggers that put me right back into that place and time. It can be the sound of keys jangling, the opening of a cell door, someone hollering, the sight or smell of blood, the drab colors of old bars, or any number of other things. Almost instantly, I am back there. I question myself about what I could have done differently. It makes no sense to me. Who is going to come back and kill someone the same day the ultimatum is delivered? Maybe they come back to knock him around, show they are serious, but to murder him? How does that work? And what did his life even mean at that point? What was it worth under those circumstances? They should have killed me too, but they made yet another mistake. We will remember that day in different ways, but time will erode everything. In a hundred years, no one will know or remember anything.

No Exit from Hell

IN the coming days, weeks, months, and years, I will be forced to go through absolute hell because of this one event. Nearly every day there will be some consequence, some memory, or some feeling that is directly connected to that one event on that one day of my life. I will be manipulated, lied on, and threatened. Nothing will come out the way it is supposed to because everything has been thrown out-of-whack. Some will hail me while others will vilify me. I am already a pariah, for there is a standing contract on my life and my name is well- known in the federal system. My mind will do what it does outside of my control and will produce all sort of feelings I do not understand.

There is a dark cloud of death, destruction, and despair that hangs over my head and follows me around. I have been beaten, chained, spit upon, humiliated, and abused in many other ways, but I am not bitter. The prosecutors used me to get their high-profile convictions and promotions and then threw me under the bus. The prisoncrats hate me because I escaped their grasp for a time and embarrassed them. The prisoners hate me because I went against their notions of criminality. And all of this is due to that one fateful day when I tried to save my friend's life and failed. It was a bad day for both of us for all of us, but I would do it all over again because I never had a choice.

Layers and layers of confinement: chains and gates and keys and doors and locks and bars and sticks and cuffs and razor wire and towers and gas and fences and walls and guns and bullets. It is sheer overkill. Someone has been watching too many movies. There is no way to escape from this place. It cannot be done. I am at the bottom of a deep pit, a labyrinth of concrete and steel, a gauntlet of legal obfuscation. This is hell warmed over. I am a zombie that wanders from one day to the next with no purpose other than to feed. I am confined in a cage that is within a cage that is within a cage. I am being kept by human beings, and it seems like the movie "Planet of the Apes." The only way I get fresh air is to write these words.

> *I am parked in a stolen car, waiting for certain family members to come home. I have just escaped from a maximum-security federal prison, and I have done what they always say not to in going back home. As I wait, an elderly woman across the street comes out with a push mower and tries to start it. I watch for a few minutes and then get out to go help her. I end up mowing her entire lawn, front and back, and it is the best! The sun is on my back, the mower is humming right along, and I am working*

in relative freedom. No one is telling me what to do, or touching me, or trying to harm me. It may be just a lawn to some, but to me it is paradise.

In the past, I thought about how to escape this place. I thought there must be a way if I could only see it. These were all a product of wishful thinking. In the past, I thought that my appeals in the courts would be successful. Surely a federal judge would notice my plight and give me some kind of relief, but that was insanity to believe. If I completed the sentences, how old would I be when I was finally released? Oh, too old. And what exactly would be the quality of life for me during the more advanced years? Would I need to use a walker? Would I need to wear adult diapers? What the hell did it all mean?

What is on the outside of these walls? People going about their daily routines, working, communicating, watching TV, having sex, getting a bite to eat somewhere... Commercialization and the search and rescue of the Almighty Dollar is ruling everyone. No one seems to be living the kind of life promised. It looks like a lot of pain and loneliness and misery going on out there. The news is never good news, and freedom is not all it is cracked up to be. Here I am living free of charge. I pay nothing except what is pried from my impoverished soul. Is it not true that those who are on the other side of that wall over there are also confined.

It simply makes no sense to me anymore to think about escape. Escape to what, another prison cell. Nonetheless, the guards take no chances with me. They honestly believe I will pull a Houdini on them and simply vanish. They are paranoid as can be, afraid for their jobs. They listen in via the intercom that is mounted inside the sally port or at least they think they do.

But recently I was able to use a contraption I made to loosen the screws on the plate and, thereafter, disconnected the wires. They still conduct cell searches every day or two, and they chain me up pretty tightly any time they remove me from the cell. It is constantly astounding that any legislative body would approve the kind of funding it must require to implement these over-the-top security measures.

It seems like there is no end in sight. There is no light at the end of this tunnel only a darker and deeper hole. I am wasting away in this cage, the life running out on me. Each day seems to be an exact duplicate of the one that came before it. I am trying

64

*not to be negative, but the reality is too powerful. Life in a cage
is the equivalent of no life at all. It is sinister. Do other human
beings really have a right to keep me here like this? For what?
Where are the premises of fairness in a biased and punitive
system like this one? These so-called authorities will blast a
hole through a prisoner's chest at 500 yards and go get a
hamburger. Is it only me, or is there something wrong with this
picture?*

It is hard to deal with human beings. We are dangerous animals who prey on one
another in a host and variety of ways. There are always two sides: the winners and
the losers. Mostly everyone wants to be on the side of the winners because they get
the rewards. The losers get the disgrace and punishment. It is a rather lame
dynamic, but it is human nature. Those who have the position, the power, the
favor, or the privilege always think they are on the right side of things. But when
they fall, they fall hard! Many of them probably end up disillusioned later on down
the road. And by then they are too far gone, too far into the throes of their own
hypocrisy to escape the effects. But in any case, it is the hardest thing to stand in
judgment of others. I am writing this as a cautionary tale that is all too true. It is
because I want people to feel what I am feeling. There is a pervasive sense of
despair that is wrapped around my heart and is squeezing. There is a certain
hopelessness in my bones the kind that makes me want to drop to my knees and
cry out in anguish and pain. My mind is fried to a crisp. It has been exposed to the
flames of this hell for too long. My story is for those who want to learn how to
love, how to cherish freedom, and how to learn from their mistakes. So, while
there may be no escape for me, there is still an escape for those who can hear me.

And as to those individuals who have taken it upon themselves by whatever artifice
they have used to cause me harm for the purposes of harm well shame on you. I
cannot lie and say have no anger, no animosity or rage. The only way to rid myself
of these terrible feelings that have been forced upon me is to mutilate myself. They
say, "Why did you do this?" It is because of what you did to me when you went
past my cell without feeding me, when you threw my mail in the trash, when you
clamped those handcuffs into the bones in my wrists, when you sprayed me in the
face with CS gas, and a million other offenses that you committed against me and
others. Yes, we are guilty of distinct crimes, but you are guilty of the continuing
crimes; we are guilty of serious crimes, but you are guilty of the worst crimes. For
you have deprived me and others of our right to be equally human.

65

It is my own blood that holds them accountable, and I will spill it on this concrete floor as an expiation. in this act, I am making the only statement I can make. It is also for those who it is not too late for those who will step into the same trap of ignorance that I stepped in, unless they are exceedingly careful. I am redeeming both them and me. In this blood is my life, and it is representative of their lives as well. Everyone has committed some wrong, and I forgive us all. If we could but meet on equal terms equal understanding in this moment, I feel we would bond together with a realization of brotherhood and common causes. But those who commit atrocities and do not repent are doomed because they have ignored this moment.

The Shadow of Death

THE new psychologist comes around and says she is going to have the guards pull me out so we can talk. I like her and I feel a need to talk to someone who is neither a guard nor a prisoner. So I get myself together, tidy up my papers and books, and wait to go out. It is nothing but an empty room downstairs next to the officer's station that is used as a barber shop. I will be put in there, the chains will be removed, and the slot in the door will be left open. I will squat down so that I am eye level with the slot, and the psychologist will sit in a chair just outside, in the hallway. The guards show up to get me hooked up, checked, searched, waned, et cetera.

PSYCHOLOGIST: Do you think there are people who care about you?

POWERS: Yeah, I think so.

PSYCHOLOGIST: Do you think that if you kill yourself that they will be sad?

POWERS: Yeah, they would be.

PSYCHOLOGIST: Do you think your life might have some meaning or purpose that isn't apparent right now?

POWERS: Maybe. But there is nothing special about me.

PSYCHOLOGIST: Why do you think you keep harming yourself? Is it for attention or to get something you want?

POWERS: Probably both of those but not in the way you think. I do want to draw attention to the unfair treatment of prisoners here, including myself, and I do want changes made.

PSYCHOLOGIST: What happens if you inadvertently kill yourself as a result of some self-harm?

POWERS: No big loss. There are what, seven or eight billion people on this planet.

PSYCHOLOGIST: I think you get angry or bored or impulsive and play Russian roulette. You seem to be ambivalent about whether you live or die, and that is understandable given your circumstances.

It has been a good session. I feel better for having communicated with someone who is somewhat sympathetic to my circumstances. It is like having someone on my side for once. I am waiting for the guards to come get me and bring me back to my cell. They seem to be doing something on the ranges, and it takes them a while to come for me. They chain me up tightly, hands and feet, and open the door. As soon as I turn to go up the stairs, they pull me back and tell me: "We went ahead and moved you to a new cell over on B-range while you were talking to the psych." My whole body goes rigid with electricity, for I do not want to move to B-range.

POWERS: You moved my stuff?

GUARD: It's all in your new cell.

POWERS: But I don't want to move to B-range. I want to stay where I was.

GUARD: Too bad you don't make those choices, Powers.

POWERS: Well, who ordered this?

GUARD: It came from above my head.

POWERS: You know this is not going to turn out well for any of us, right?

GUARD: I know! Doesn't matter, though. You do what you feel you need to.

Powers is standing in the new cell on B-range. They guards have removed the restraints and are signaling for the outer door to be closed. Everyone knows there will be a reaction, and they are in a hurry to leave the range. Powers looks at the pile of papers and books on the floor and a new wave of intense anger sweeps over him. They have poured coffee over everything. It is too much for Powers to accept, and he goes ballistic! He uses an encyclopedia to smack down flat on the concrete TV shelf until it cracks and breaks. He now uses this piece of concrete to smash out the back window. It shatters into thousands of pieces. Then he begins throwing everything every piece of property in the cell out the window.

Powers is far beyond any semblance of control. He uses pieces of the broken glass to slash his arms and sprays blood all over the cell's walls, ceiling and floor. He eats a handful of glass and spits blood. The guards, hearing the commotion, have come down the range and are standing by the outer door. They are watching Powers as he sits by the window, bleeding profusely. They wait for the arrival of the lieutenant, and the lieutenant calls for a team to be assembled. It takes another ten or fifteen minutes for the guards to get suited up in their protective gear. Then they line up in the hallway by the door. The door opens and they run inside the cell and tackle Powers and drag him out.

> *The loss of blood has weakened me. Otherwise I would have fought them tooth and nail. They dragged me into the hallway and held me down until someone from medical came to wrap my arms with gauze bandages to staunch the bleeding. Medical proceeded to cut my clothes off of me, and then I was dragged down the hallway and over to another special cell on a-range. They left me in that cell with all of the chains still on me. There was nothing in the cell no mattress, no blanket, no clothing, no nothing. so as soon as they left I got a drink of water and went to work on getting the chains off of me.*

I use the horizontal flat steel on the inner bars to jam between the metal of the handcuffs where they hinge. Then I work them up and down until the rivet holding the cuffs together breaks. I do the same to the other one and then begin on the leg-irons, which are more difficult. I work the belly chain down and over my waist and legs, and now I am free of the chains. I use the chains to bust out the back window and fresh air floods the cell. It is evening and it is dark outside. I breathe in the air and watch the sky. Doors are being opened and the demons will be back soon, so I swallow another handful of glass and wash it down with water from the tap in the sink. The water tastes good, and I drink too much of it.

> *I had forgotten that it was the beginning of easter weekend and that the normal administrative staff were gone until Monday. There is a dyed in the wool, 24 carat, bona fide asshole lieutenant who has been left to run the place, and he is none too*

happy about what I am doing. He sends yet another team in on me. They gas me and come in on me. Naked and barely able to breathe or see, I tried to fight them off. They got me down and pummeled me. Then, at the lieutenant's directions, they carried me to another area of the prison where they have a room that has a raised concrete platform in the center of the floor. The lieutenant ordered them to hold me face down while others applied tight chains to hold me in place, naked, on the slab. They put chains across my back, four or five on both arms and on both legs and tighten them so that I cannot move an inch in any direction.

After several days of being chained down like this, Powers is in extremis. He is dehydrated and his entire body has been subject to the force of the chains. The lieutenant has been around on several different occasions. He brings a video camera and other staff members. It is like he is showing off his work. Powers cannot breathe because his chest cannot expand properly. The weight of the chains is too much. There must be seventy-five pounds of chains altogether. Powers has not been given water or food or medical treatment. He has been forced to urinate and defecate in place, and none of it has been cleaned up. The staff laugh and make fun of Powers from an observation window.

Powers is standing at the edge of a deep dark pit that goes so far down he cannot see if there is a bottom. The pit is drawing everything around it like a giant vacuum cleaner: cars, trees, trash, and all kinds of debris. Powers is hanging on, struggling against the pull, but he is in peril of being dragged into the pit. The terrible shadow of death is upon him now, and the feeling is beyond description. A strange looking animal unfolds itself in the corner of the cell and crawls over to lick his hand. The smell of it is horrid. Then someone is in the room, behind Powers and unseen. It is someone cleaning the urine and feces. Then Powers experiences a sharp stabbing pain in his testicles. He screams out in a feeble and parched scream. The pain is so intense that it makes powers begin to cry. There are no tears, but he cannot stop crying.

Powers has been babbling, pleading and crying. He is hallucinating and has decompensated to a significant degree. There are several administrators in the hallway. After a heated exchange, the guards begin to remove the chains. They sit

70

Powers up and hold him there while they dress him. They lift him into a wheelchair and roll him back down the hall to the control unit. He is placed in a barren and stripped cell with only a mattress. The wounds on his arms are infected. There are lacerations around his ankles and wrists when the restraints were applied much too tightly. He tries to stand and finds that he cannot, so he crawls to a corner of the cell and hunches down there. He is shivering uncontrollably and cannot stop himself from crying in short but intense bursts.

There is no good way for anyone to recover from the effects of torture. The body may or may not recover, but the mind itself never does. The extent of degradation and abuse at the hands of another human being is too much to process. It is simply inconceivable, and it changes the entire paradigm. It reveals a dark reality about the animals called human and how cruel they are beneath the façade of being civilized. People have tortured people in the most horrific ways for thousands of years, and it will continue. There is no answer or remedy for such a thing. It is much worse when it is so called authorities because the underpinning of that authority proves to be false. Those who commit such acts are by far the worst criminals among mankind.

Nice to be Dead

THIS is what a penitentiary Warden might say when addressing the executive staff:

"To some of the do-gooders outside of the prison environment it may seem that we use barbaric methods to keep order inside our prisons. But they do not work inside a prison, and they have no idea what it takes to keep the public safe. We are those who are charged with the care, custody, and control of convicted felons. And please bear in mind that these inmates are not in prison for being late to Sunday school.......

"The majority of these offenders have been found guilty of having committed serious crimes against our society. They do this because they are criminals. The fact is, they do not stop being criminals or stop committing crimes just because they are in prison. If anything, their criminality becomes even worse. Many of them have nothing to lose, and a good number of them actually want to be in prison.

"Sometimes we must use force in order to maintain control of the institution or to protect the lives and safety of staff and inmates and to prevent escapes. We try our best to avoid the use of force, but our best efforts do not always succeed. And when it becomes necessary to use force, we only use the amount of force that is needed. We do not use force as punishment because that would be against the law. Inmates do become aggressive, and when they do, we must take action.

"Remember that inmates are dangerous. They often make weapons to use against staff or other inmates. We are not here to punish inmates, but we must protect lives and property. So, whenever there is a threat, it is our job to take action in order to regain control. Since inmates are not that good at listening to reason, we do not waste a lot of time trying to reason with them. We also never ever give in to their demands.

"Ironically, we must protect inmates against themselves, which is difficult at best. We are accountable for taking reasonable actions to prevent an inmate from harming or killing himself. Our policies represent the guidelines for what to do in certain instances, but they cannot cover every angle. There are times when we need to be proactive and even creative in our approach."

They are trying hard to break my spirit. In some ways, I think they have succeeded, for in some ways I am a broken man. They want me to accept whatever they decide to do to me without any questions or resistance. They subjected me to torture for no good reason. I did not assault anyone. I did not make or possess a weapon of any kind. I did not threaten anybody. The only thing I did, really, was to break a couple of windows. I was fed up with their bullshit! Put any kind of an animal inside a cage and keep poking it with a sharp stick and, eventually, it will snap at the stick. They wanted to show me who was boss, but they went too far. Now there is an investigation by the Inspector General's office, but these things are nearly always a white wash.

In the end there will be no accountability. My body remains bruised and battered. My testicles remain painful and swollen. My body will eventually heal up, but this episode has left me damaged in ways that far exceed what was done to my body. For a fellow human being to kill me is one thing, but to do something as sinister and diabolical as what they did to me in that room is something else altogether. In a perfect world someone would have reported such abuses to the supervisors immediately, and every one of the perpetrators would have been fired and indicted. But they will get away with it because they are twisted, and no one wants to untwist them.

> *To lie naked on a concrete slab with pounds and pounds of chains holding you down. To be stretched and twisted into a high stress position and left like that for more than a week. To be forced to shit and piss on yourself, to go without food and water. To have a fucked up, sick, sadistic son of a bitch lieutenant tormenting you and directing the guards to torture you. To suffer the agony of a physical and mental ordeal to the point where you begin to hallucinate. To have your testicles stabbed through with a syringe or a needle. To be laughed at and mocked the entire time by those who are supposed to be better than that. No one can tell me anything about right and wrong anymore.*

My testicle still has a lump where the injury occurred. It hurts a lot in that area, and I have no idea what they did to me. I am wanting to look at it to see what is wrong, so I use a purloined razor blade and cut through the skin. It takes several cuts due to the thickness of the skin there. There seems to be congealed blood inside. I use warm water with iodized salt in it to wash it away and what a mistake that proves to be! Finally, I am able to get to the testicle itself. There is a blackish lump near the spermatic cord. I hesitate for a moment and then cut with a couple of swift strokes. The testicle falls onto the floor and blood spurts and streams like nothing I have ever seen.

> *A guard making rounds has found Powers seated against the wall in his cell, nearly unconscious, with a large puddle of blood around him. He calls it in, and, within a few minutes, Powers is being taken to medical. He is trailing thick blood all the way through the hall ways. He has severed an artery one that comes off of the aorta and it has sucked up into his abdomen. The medical staff puts in an emergency I.V., hooks up an oxygen mask, and calls for an ambulance. By the time powers reaches the hospital, he is clinically dead. His blood pressure is at zero. He is operated on immediately and infused with a total of six units of blood. It is touch and go for a couple of days before Powers regains consciousness. As soon as he is declared stable, the guards rush him back to the ADX control unit.*

The days go by slowly. I am doing a lot of writing again but not much reading. The new Warden has changed our access to books by shortening our book list from about 3500 titles to about 150. It is all crime thrillers and romance. Anything that had anything to do with learning is now gone. The upshot is that I am back in my old cell over Gato now. They move us every ninety days to other cells (for security reasons) and then back again. I am still into the practice of Yoga, and the psychologist has given me great books on the subject whenever I get around to reading them. Gato and I are back to playing our version of chess via the empty sink drain.

GATO: Sounds like a herd of wild horses up there. What are you doing up there?

POWERS: Cleaning the cell. There is all kinds of crap all over the place, and I have to do something about it.

GATO: I had pictures of Puerto Rico on my shelf, but the hacks took them and tore them up when I went to rec this morning.

POWERS: It's a beautiful place, right? Puerto Rico?

GATO: It's the most beautiful place in the world. I wish I could be back there right now.

POWERS: Well, you are in a way. I mean in your mind you can be there. Why don't you make some shorts, take your shoes off, run the water in the shower, and pretend you are on the beach over there

GATO: I'll never see home again. I know that.

POWERS: Maybe that's true, but you never know for sure.

GATO: Did you have any kind of out of body thing happen when you were dead?

POWERS: Nope. Don't remember anything. It was just nothingness. Maybe your heart has to stop, and mine must have had some small life still in it.

GATO: It must be nice to be dead.

Gato's illness seems to be getting worse. He talks normally to me, but as soon as the guards come down the range, he goes off on them! He screams on them and calls them every kind of name he can think of, and then he comes back to the sink like nothing happened. Of course, they have been doing a lot of bogus shit to him for a long, long time. I cannot blame him for feeling a certain way about them. It must be equally difficult for the guards because they are hated as much as they hate. They are stuck in those roles, indoctrinated into the life, powerless to change anything. Most of them hate their jobs and do not have much of a life outside of their prison-based associations.

Sometimes I hear Gato crying when he says he is lying down. He continues to claim that the guards are coming into his cell to beat him up and rape him. He wants a phone call to his family, to his mother, and the unit manager, a pathetic imp, will not allow it. Gato is not a violent person, but he feels he needs to act like he is. It is not a good situation for him right now, and it is not likely to get much better any time soon. He has less possessions than I do, he has virtually no privileges, and he has no one to help him. There is no doubt that Gato is suffering from a serious mental illness. The fact that he receives no treatment for it is the main cause of his erratic behavior. It is a classic Catch-22.

Trixie was my dog. I got her for Christmas when I was six years old. We spent years together, roaming the woods and fields, and I loved her very much. When I started running around as a teenager, I began to neglect her. Sometimes, though, she and I would cross the highway to put pheasants to flight on the other side. I was playing foosball with some of my friends at a small pizza joint when my sister came in. She was shaking. She said she thought Trixie had been hit by a car on the highway. I went there and searched for her and found her there, in the grass by the side of the road, and she was dead. I picked her up and carried her home and buried her in the backyard under a tall pine tree.

Breaking it Down

GATO talks to himself in a weird, high pitched voice and then answers in some purposely low bass type voice. I can hear him down there carrying on with himself. At first I thought he was talking to an orderly or to a staff member, but that was not the case. He says things that makes no sense whatsoever and, when I question him about them, he denies having said them. I thought he was messing with my head, but as time has passed I see that he is virtually insane. He is extremely paranoid, delusional, and dissociated, but the staff and psychology think he is faking. If he is faking, he is doing one hell of a job of it because he has totally convinced me.

I have been working on a project I want to leave to posterity. It is a short work entitling The Crystalline Doctrine. It is a set of fundamental insights I have realized while in here, and I have tried to render a poetic effect in answering questions that are common to humans. I also want to develop some kind of a more comprehensive course on character building. The main goal I have is to create something that will be useful in terms of helping others to better themselves. I am fully awry of the many flaws I have in my own character, and I want to find a way to correct them, if possible. I have been reading a lot about personal growth and development, personal transformation, and the steps to enlightenment. They are all the same things being said in different ways. It makes me feel better about wasting away in this hellhole of a prison.

I too am having more difficulties. The relentless antagonism is taking a toll. Now that I have taken up for Gato, the guards have doubled down in their harassment campaign against me. The only person who has taken up for me is the new psychologist. She has stood in their way fearlessly on a number of occasions, and they hate her. They always make her wait, and they make fun of her behind her back. She will not last too much longer because they, the shirts at the top of this heap, will run her off. I feel that I am simply biding my time until the day comes when I know I am ready to go all out to make certain I make my exit permanent.

The captain comes to the cell front with several guards in tow. He radios and tells control to open the outer door. He and a couple of the guards come into the sally port. The captain says he needs to pull me out. They take me downstairs to the same room where I talk to the psychologist. They have me sit in a chair, and they surround me. The chaplain from the F.C.I. comes into the room. He has a postcard or letter in his hand. He says he has some bad news for me, and he tells me that my little brother has died. I guess they expect me to have some violent reaction, but I tell him thanks for relaying the message and ask to be taken back to the cell.

Somehow we need to help one another. We must be able and willing to give and receive in equal proportions. We need bona fide methods of self-realization. The main idea is to care enough about ourselves and our fellow human beings to do no harm.

If people can be genuine in this regard, society will prosper. The problem is the perception that some people are better than others. We constantly judge ourselves and others by meaningless comparisons. But we are all members of the human race, and we are all equally human beings. Our best power is in the unity of our actions, so let us do right by one another. Each person can play a significant role in moving this thing forward. In some instances it may be difficult to avoid conflict, but cooperation is superior because it builds up as opposed to tearing down.

Powers has come to the place where he is ready. He has decided to cut the blood vessels in his arms and sit down until he bleeds out. He has it planned for Friday night when the guards are not paying much attention to anything on the ranges. He is not planning on telling Gato anything about it because Gato is barely lucid these days. He goes about getting together the few little items he wants or needs. He has a small piece of a razor blade that he attaches a plastic handle to; he has a candle already; he has his final papers neatly bound and sitting on the TV stand.

It is a combination of events that has brought me to this point. I have gone over the edge and am not about to come back. There is nothing left to hold me back. I am scared at first, maybe apprehensive, but after I bleed a while I begin to feel better. There is a statement I want to make with my death. suicide has been on my mind so much lately that I need to listen and understand. The mental anguish is only when you are up against death and have no choice in the matter. You begin to feel like you have a secret, and it is liberating to know you are finally going to come to a conclusion. I always wondered what my state of mind might be when my life is gushing out of deep cuts in my arms. It is more of a resignation, an acceptance of a bitter pill. I have been driven out of this world, but I am glad to

be going. this is not my kind of place. at least I get to choose the
time and place, and I have chosen now.

There are many things that must have happened that Powers knows nothing about. It is days or weeks or months or years after the fact, and still there are pieces missing. Only one thing is sure: Powers is still alive, and he is very much discouraged. He thinks himself an unlucky loser. It is a terrible predicament he is in--worse than before he bled out. How could he still be alive after losing so much blood? What kind of sick game is being played here? Powers needed to die! He wanted to be gone, and he did everything right to make it happen. What went wrong?

> UNIT MANAGER: Hey, Powers. I'm your new unit manager. I saw the photos of your cell. It looked like

> ten people had bled out in there. Lucky we found you when we did. You were all but gone.

> POWERS: I don't know what you mean. How could I be lucky? How could you be lucky? We are all going to die anyway.

> CASE MANAGER: We are going to send you down to Springfield for another evaluation. Frankly, you are scaring the hell out of us. We don't want your blood on our hands.

> POWERS: Kill myself someplace else, is what you're saying. But does it make any difference? A hundred years from now no one will know the difference. It's all a waste of time another trip through the spin cycle.

> CASE MANAGER: Well, I'm only concerned about the here and now. I am hoping you will cooperate with the eval and get the help you need. As long as you continue to cause us problems, you will be kept in the control unit.

> POWERS: You sound like a pompous asshole.

When things go bad here, they go bad quickly. This is another major disappointment on top of my incredibly intense despair. Off to Springfield again! What a waste of time. It is what the feds do to twist the screws in yet another way. This is not to help me not at all. This transfer is going to be pure punishment. Springfield is a worse shithole than the ADX! It should have been bulldozed a hundred years ago. It is all witches, goblins, and demons that assemble around that portal. It is my punishment for failure. Another round of bullshit quacks, hacks, and assholes. Maybe this will teach me a good lesson. Next time I will hang myself. The prisoners who hang themselves always succeed.

Those poor bastards at Springfield really are crazy. They live in squalor and unsanitary conditions. If not for the application of lots of medications, they would either kill themselves or riot. It is a terrible mess there. They kept Gato at Springfield for a long time but ultimately decided that he was not crazy at all. It is always the same drivel: antisocial personality and malingering. Prisoners typically go there to rot in hell. But to allow them to label you as having any mental illness is even worse. Now they can yank your ass around any way they want to and get away with it under the cover of involuntary treatment. Once they take a prisoner through the kangaroo court and get the judge to rubber stamp a commitment order, that prisoner is absolutely finished. Prisoners fight and scream and cry, but they are always forcefully subdued and given that injection. After that, they just remain on the bunk, laying there, staring off into space. They are never themselves again after that.

The entirety of prison life is a masquerade that plays out on a hidden and superficial stage. Who can know what occurs behind the scenes. There is a sparsity of sensible solutions. The words and ideals are separated from the base realities of human beings living a human life. No one knows anything. We have all kinds of words that sound good to throw around, but it is anyone's guess as to what is really going on. There are ten times as many questions as there are answers to them, for every question multiplies itself. It is a constant dynamic between those who are on one side of the door and those who are on the other side of the door. To automatically assume the upper hand is sometimes a mistake. It is a dance an exchange of intangible intentions.

There are those who think Powers is only making trouble to have something to do with his time, but this is called cognitive indolence on their part. Things will change and Powers will come through. It will take time, of course, but time is no longer of the essence. Powers is on his own time, and he is making things happen within the context of his own heart and mind. He is no longer uncertain about his destiny; it has all been worked out. Anyone who surmises the course of his future is likely to be wrong. He himself has no definitive idea, and the less he speculates the better he feels about it. The pieces that have broken off and are gone were not the essential pieces.

The Lights Go Out

THE prisoner's life is one that is not conducive to friendship, for how can a true friendship develop? Movement, capabilities, personalities, forms, hunger, thirst, morbid curiosity, and lights. Always lights. They are all over the place. Some of the guards have fancy flashlights that have a variety of features. They are powerful like a spotlight that they hold on to your face while you are trying to sleep. Am I sleeping or awake now? It is hard to say because day is night and whatever used to pass for reality is now unreal. Has anyone ever discovered where words come from or what they mean? It occurs to me that words are all that connect us; they are all that makes friendship possible. We are all nobodies who are trying desperately to be somebodies. Gato is dead, and the lights have gone out.

It is a Saturday morning, and I am writing a letter to the Warden about Gato's predicament and the way he is being mistreated. I have written many other letters and have never received a reply, but this does not stop me from writing more. It is quiet on the range. At around count time, there is some loud radio traffic and keys jangling. Doors clank open and closed and footsteps of guards who are in a hurry sound in the hallway. This is not out of the ordinary. The outer door of my cell suddenly cranks open and a woman with curlers in her hair comes into the sally port. She is an internal affairs investigator, and I wonder what she is doing here on a Saturday at this time of the morning with curlers in her hair. The sun is shining outside the window, but it is not shining the way it should be. All of the lights on the range go out and the guards get back on their radios.

> INVESTIGATOR: Hey, Powers. I need to ask you a couple of questions about Jose Vega.

> POWERS: Gato? They moved him to another cell yesterday afternoon after the guards provoked him into throwing something on them. I'm writing to the Warden right now.

> INVESTIGATOR: Vega is dead. He hanged himself this morning. Did he say anything to you about wanting to kill himself?

> POWERS: Not really. I mean, he made some comments at times that could be interpreted one way or the other, but that's fairly common in here.

> INVESTIGATOR: Sure.

POWERS: You folks didn't think this would happen? All the harassment and torment? The complete lack of care for his mental health? You come to investigate now after the fact and expect what, to convince me that you are surprised it happened?

INVESTIGATOR: I need to move on, Powers. If you hear anything shoot me a cop-out.

POWERS: Ask them (the guards) to turn the lights out.

It seems that I am happy for Gato but sad for me. The day did not feel right to begin with. Everything was off. Gato was doing all right yesterday right up until he went off on the guards. They were bringing him back from recreation and must have said or did something. Maybe he already had it planned. Who knows? There was some loud and profane exchanges and then a silence that was punctuated by Gato laughing. He would not answer when I tried to talk with him. A few minutes later, they came back to get him. They used the team and a force cell move, and he was gone. I am happy for him. He got out. There was no way he was going to have anything except more misery. In my book, he is now in a better place.

In contrast, the guards are hush-hush about the whole thing, and for good reason. They could be in serious trouble if the truth comes out. They will be on pins and needles for a few days, and then they will go back to doing their thing. It is basically, good ridden to a piece-of-shit inmate. No one is going to lose much sleep over it. There will be some perfunctory investigation, and then it will all be swept under the carpet and forgotten. There is no outside organization that is willing to address this matter. Gato is not the first prisoner to kill himself, and there are certain to be more who will on down the road. It is another tragedy added to a long litany of tragedies.

There is a smell like blood. there are remnants of my blood in the cracks and crevices. Gato was in ambulatory restraints when he killed himself. There are more than a few who are questioning whether he killed himself or whether the guards killed him. It was not the guards. Apparently, Gato got his shirt off and tied it to the bars. He put his head into the loop and leaned backward. The shirt squeezed on both sides of his neck and cut off the flow of blood to his brain. He went unconscious within seconds and was brain dead within five minutes. Pursuant to policy, they left the restraints on him throughout

the trip to a local hospital and, from there, to the morgue. It
was a quick and painless death. It takes a lot of courage to end
your own life, and Gato prevailed in his quest for relief. His
death was not in vain.

The guards bang on the cell door to wake me up when they see me resting. The inmate next cell down keeps blowing the circuit, and the lights keep going out. I feel responsible for Gato's death. It was my own statements and attempts that gave him the idea. He told me he had freaked out the night I bled myself out. The blood had even gone down the crack in the back wall and into his cell. There were things I could have said and done to stop him, but I would have only been extending his pain. I am lonely now without him around. It makes me think of Eddie and I wonder why I am here, and they are gone.

We are kids taking a hike through the cow pastures when we
hear a raucous noise coming from the woods nearby. In
another moment or two we see a big crow flying low to the
ground. There are a bunch of smaller birds flying with the
crow, attacking it from every angle, and ripping out a bunch of
feathers. The crow has a desperate look of fear in its eyes and
is clearly fatigued. the smaller birds do not show any mercy
whatsoever to the crow. They are relentless as they take turns
snatching feathers.

Powers cannot breathe. The air in the cell is stale and stifling. He is nauseated and feels sick. He gets up and looks out of the window and sees the night sky looking fresh and clear. He strikes the window three times with his fist before it breaks. The reason it breaks so easily is because it is designed that way. It is too narrow to get in or out of, but prison officials must have wanted a means of gassing prisoners from the outside. The fresh air is a great relief! Powers lies back down and keeps his head close to the broken window. He hopes that the guards will not notice it for a day or two. It is most likely that they will.

Powers comes awake an hour or two later. He sits up suddenly. He looks out the window and listens to the soft sound of the night. He looks at his hands and spreads his fingers, closing and opening them. The pinkie finger has healed nicely. He puts it into his mouth and clamps down on it with his teeth. He does not let off until the joint is severed, and the finger is spurting blood. He spits it out the window and lies back down. He is able to sleep soundly and awakens at breakfast time with the remnants of a vivid dream still affecting him.

PSYCHOLOGIST: You did it again! Come on! I thought we were making progress.

POWERS: Yeah, when I broke the window the air hit me, and I began to get depressed. Next thing I knew, the finger was gone.

PSYCHOLOGIST: What did you do with it?

POWERS: Spit it out the window, Let the birds have it.

PSYCHOLOGIST: They might have been able to reattach it, you know.

POWERS: That's all right. I wasn't using it for anything anyway.

PSYCHOLOGIST: Did you ingest any of the glass?

POWERS: Not this time. Last time was a mistake, let me tell you. It hurts coming out.

PSYCHOLOGIST: Where does this go now?

POWERS: Who knows? I am just riding the waves, trying to figure it all out just like you are.

PSYCHOLOGIST: Are you still practicing yoga?

POWERS: Yes, in fact. It has helped me a great deal. The world we live in is not nice, you know. It does not fit into a neat little box with a bow on it.

PSYCHOLOGIST: I know.

A certain numbness has set in. I am an automaton, a zombie. I get my food trays and sit down on the edge of the bunk to eat. The food has no taste to it, and I rarely eat it all. It is all too true that I have lost a good deal of motivation. I do not read or write much anymore. Usually, I sit and just sort of blank out. My mind refuses to process thought or emotion. I am like the sink or the toilet fixture in the cell. The days go past, but I am unable to tell one from another. I had another vivid dream where someone came to me. I am not sure who it was some yogi I presume. He was marked with tattoos from head to toe, and he breathed on me like the air that came through the broken window.

A New Asylum

THE Director of the Federal Bureau of Prisons comes around every few years or so. They have a big dog-and-pony show and lay it on thick. I can only imagine what the director is saying to the executive staff in Washington, D.C.:

"Our prisons and jails are becoming insane asylums. Each year we see an increase in the number of inmates who have serious mental health issues. We do not have the resources to provide the treatment they require so we usually put them in solitary confinement and leave them there for as long as we can. As the mental hospitals around the country have closed, those who ordinarily end up at those facilities now end up in prison. It is a major challenge for everyone involved.

"Correctional facilities as I'm sure you know are places where the structure and the rules are paramount to the security and orderly running of the institution. Those who have mental illness are also incapable of following the rules at times. Additionally, many of them are victimized by the other inmates and may commit some act to be placed in segregation where they feel safe. Some experts estimate that there are a couple of hundred thousand prisoners who have a serious mental illness. The numbers are overwhelming.

"Mental illness is not only one thing; it is several things, and these general categories also have their own divisions. One of them is called psychosis. This includes schizophrenia and other disorders where there is paranoia, delusional thoughts, and associated symptoms. These inmates are usually not dangerous as long as they are taking their medications, but they can go completely off the rails when they aren't. Those inmates who have stress and anxiety disorders are much more likely to become violent in a prison setting. They are also much more likely to commit suicide or self-mutilation.

"For the most part, treatment consists of therapy and medications administered within a stable, safe, and goal-oriented environment. The psychologist develops a treatment plan, which might include a psychiatric consult, for each inmate. As you can see, these components are not typically available within a prison. All of this extra care is quite costly and does not share the same penological goals as are current in our system. We are not receiving the funding to meet these demands, so we do the best we can with what we have."

The same being appeared again in a dream. He unfolded a piece of paper that had a lot of what looked like Sanskrit writing on it. But the writing was in a design that looked like a hybrid human cat creature or something. I have made a similar drawing and it looks like a pattern of symbols. I have the idea to tattoo the pattern onto my body, starting at my feet and working my way up until I get to the top of my head. I have been burning carbon paper in the shower to get the ashes. I have small pieces of glass left over from the broken windows and can use those to make micro-incisions in my skin. Then I can simply rub the ashes into the incisions, and it will take. The thing that I have failed to realize ahead of time is the fact that the carbon paper I am burning has poisonous chemicals in it. I am making a lot of progress with the tattoos, but after I do a section I have to lie down. I wrap up in blankets and shiver and shake for hours before falling asleep. When I get up again, I go right back to the work at hand. It has been relatively easy so far. Tattooing the back of my legs, buttocks, and back will be a challenge. I will need to use a mirror and make a pole of some sort to reach with. There may not always be a means of getting something done, but usually there is when it is broken down into small steps.

The guard comes around early in the morning. He has control open the outer door and steps inside the sally port. He tells me that there is an executive panel meeting scheduled. I am still under the blanket, and I say that I will get up and get ready. I have been up late last night applying the tattoos to my face and head. I look like an avatar. When the guards come back to get me, they see that my entire body is covered with tattoos. I expect them to say something, but they only look at each other and say nothing. On the way down the stairs I see a lieutenant standing by the door to the room where the panel meets. He asks my escorts what all those marks are on my face and arms, and they tell him it is probably something I drew on with an ink pen.

DIRECTOR: What are all those marking on you? What is that?

POWERS: It's a design that came to me in a dream after Vega killed himself.

DIRECTOR: (to Warden) What is he doing back there?

WARDEN: Powers, what are you doing back there? (To guards) What is this? What are these marks on him?

GUARD: It's all over his arms and legs and even on his back. It looks like he put it on with a pen.

DIRECTOR: (to guard) It's on his back? How can he reach his back?

GUARD: We do see him practicing yoga in his cell. (Shrugs and looks around) Otherwise, I don't know.

WARDEN: (to guards) Did anyone know about this before this morning? I hope your answer is no.

GUARD: No, we had no idea. We thought it was from an ink pen. He can probably wash it off.

DIRECTOR: It looks like pen ink to me. When you get back to your cell, wash that off.

On the way back I explained to the guards that it is permanent tattoos, but they did not believe me. They waited in the sally port while I demonstrated that it would not wash off. They left out, muttering something to each other. The feeling of being vindicated swept over me and lifted my spirits. It is a great feeling to thwart their control freak mentalities and to see their faces when they realize there is nothing they can do about it. I could not help feeling elated. In my way of thinking at that time, it was a tribute to Gato and his courage. Whatever it was, the Warden decided to let me have a TV shortly thereafter. It probably killed him to do it, but it is most likely that the director suggested it.

The problem with the TV is that nearly every channel depicts some kind of rape, kidnapping, murder, rip-off, mass killing, torture, robbery or other mayhem. Great. Lock a prisoner in a cage and fill his head with these kinds of images, story lines, and depictions. I end up unplugging it most of the time and putting it underneath the shelf so I can write. I really want to smash it but have been holding myself back. There are a couple of programs I do like to watch, but I am convinced that I got more out of not having it. I like to stay busy working on my own projects and being creative. I do not want all that trash dumped into my head. What little sense I do have left I am trying to keep......

It is the time for sentencing in my bank robbery case. The judge is old and sickly and is taking a lot of medications. He looks at me with rheumy eyes. Since I have exercised my right to a trial by jury I will receive a harsher sentence than if I had cooperated and pleaded guilty. I try to think of myself as a good person who took a chance and got caught. But the truth is, I have committed a lot of crimes and have gotten away with the vast majority of them. I am not necessarily a violent person, but I am a criminal. My character is bent all out of shape. It is now time to pay the piper, as they say. the assistant U.S. Attorney hates my guts as he should because I was less than easy to deal with. So he will not be making any positive recommendations. The hearing is quick and solemn. The Judge sentences me to the maximum sentences allowable and wishes he could give me more. I am not sad because I know I deserve it. The thing that bothers me most is knowing in my heart that I should be a better person than I am.

There is a law firm up in Denver that wants to send a lawyer down here to talk to me. Apparently they want to investigate the lack of treatment for mental health disorders. Somehow they came across my name. It will be a formidable task. These prisoncrats will shake them off like a dog shakes water off its back! And I am not even sure they will allow me to have a visit in the first place. I am on restriction for just about forever. The administration will sandbag any such possibility, bury it in regulations and paperwork. Besides, the firm is not saying much about what exactly it wants to do or hopes to accomplish.

There are all kinds of precautions used whenever a prisoner at the ADX has a visitor. Everything about the visitor is closely scrutinized by investigators; prior arrangements weeks in advance are mandatory; there is a lot of high-level approval required; any visitor must pass background and security checks. If the person still wants to visit after all of that, he or she will be subjected to searches, scanners, and monitoring. It is likely easier to enter Fort Knox's gold vaults. Every visit takes place within small concrete rooms divided by thick sheets of safety glass. The prisoner remains chained, black boxed, and shackled throughout the visit. There are numerous surveillance cameras and microphones that are recording every twitch of an eyelid or silent fart.

The work on my character-building course is coming along nicely. I have noticed that all of the truly great men and women of history demonstrated a lot of the same ideas and behaviors. These break down to what I refer to as the qualities and skills of the human personality. Some of them may seem like they come naturally, but they do not. It might be easier for some people to cultivate certain qualities and skills, but they still have to be cultivated to some degree. in the absence of this cultivation, human beings tend to demonstrate the basic animal instincts that are common to all mammals. I am working on breaking it down to a method that I can use on myself to improve my personal character. I need it for myself; and if it works for me, it will work for another who are similarly situated.

Turning a Corner

THE Guard's voice comes over the intercom and tells me I have a visit. I ask who it is, but the guard ignores me. After a little while, they come onto the range to get me. They strip-search me carefully and put me in full restraints. The chains and shackles are so tight I can barely walk in them. I have to shuffle along at a slow rate of speed. It takes a long time to get to where the visiting rooms are, and the long shuffle leaves me winded. I have to give my name and number to someone behind a one-way glass. A gate opens and I am escorted to one of the visiting areas. I see two people on the other side of the glass. One of them is a tall dude with long hair and granny eyeglasses, and the other is a woman who is smartly dressed.

LAWYER: Are you John J. Powers?

POWERS: Yes I am. And you are?

LAWYER: Call me Ed. And this is my secretary who will be taking notes. The law firm I work for is interested in investigating whether there are grounds to bring a lawsuit regarding the lack of treatment for prisoners who have serious mental health disorders.

POWERS: You do know that everything we say is being recorded, right?

LAWYER: I'm sure it is, but that is one of the many hurdles we will need to deal with as we move forward.

POWERS: You do realize that this is the federal government you are dealing with. They do not play nice and the field they play on is tilted in their favor.

LAWYER: (removes eyeglasses) Our firm is one of the largest and most powerful law firms in the world, and we do not take case we can't win.

POWERS: I am only concerned about you starting something that can't be finished and making things worse than they are now.

LAWYER: I understand your concerns. We are connected all the way to the top, and we will do everything that needs to be done.

POWERS: Well then, what do you want to know?

LAWYER: Why don't you start at the beginning. Tell us you came to be here at the ADX in the first place and what has happened since you got here......

This Lawyer seems to be serious. He has heard a lot of the horror stories about this place, and the firm he works for is prestigious and powerful. He wants to force important changes in the policies and practices of the Federal Bureau of Prisons. This will, of course require a lot of investigation, litigation, and negotiation, I am sure. I told them that I am on board with them. I told them my story. I told them everything they wanted to know. My main interest is similar to theirs: improving the state of confinement for those who have serious mental health disorders. They are also going to look into Gato's circumstances and see if they can build a cause of action on that mess. I like them. They seem to be personable and deeply concerned. Moreover, they seem to be professional.

People need to get a better understanding. It is not that anyone has all the answers, but there are those who have experience, knowledge, and wisdom. There are large pieces of the puzzle that have gone missing in everyone's life. It is a challenge of ideas and concepts and principles. The goal is to successfully navigate the setbacks that can derail a person's quest for achievement. Notice how animals in the wild use every ability they have in conjunction with every opportunity they have. They are always alert and aware of their surroundings. They are always cautious. This is why kids need the training, modeling and interventions by responsible adults who can maintain certain standards that represent good character.

Those who make a living by keeping other human beings in cages and by judging them are poor examples. They do not want to lose their source of income or their power over others. All of the guards and administrators here fall into a category of people who have marginalized themselves. They often lobby for more prisons, longer sentences, and expanded laws. They have an interest in fighting criminal justice reforms and, therefore, a conflict between maintaining their livelihood and supporting rehabilitation. They have unions whose representatives go to Washington, D.C., to put pressure on lawmakers and to hire lobbyists. They link together with other law enforcement agencies to create political clout, and they have been wildly successful.

My family is visiting a local zoo. I have lingered behind inside
a small building that has thick glass and enclosures on each
side. There are lions and monkeys and tropical birds on

display. But the attention of everyone who is inside the
building is focused on a huge ape named "coco." the entire
building shakes as coco pounds the thick glass with both fists.
he is enraged! It seems that he could actually break through
the glass and attack all of us. I am pretty scared because I am
right in front of his enclosure. Coco's eyes are red and present
a fury that is beyond anything I could know or understand.
Some people are trying to get him even more riled up. Coco
looks down at me for a second and something passes between
us something primal and terrible and sad.

The majority of people who are in prisons and jails across this country are minorities. These are people who were disadvantaged by their upbringing, their immediate environment, the criminal justice system, and their own cognition or lack of it. Very little of their time in jail or prison is productive. In fact, their experiences are often counterproductive. The state and federal governments spend a lot of money to imprison them, but then they toss them into cages and leave them to their own devices. The only thing that long term confinement produces is called institutionalization. Prisoners get used to being dehumanized. They get used to being kept. They get used to the predictable routine. A good number of prisoners do not even want to leave prison after they have become used to it.

LAWYER: This has the potential to become a landmark case. It is sure to change the way the BOP treats prisoners who have mental illness. We want to use your story to generate public awareness of this issue. As you can imagine, there are not too many people who sympathize with prisoners. Your story is unique because you have no violence to speak of and no history of mental illness prior to being placed in prison.

POWERS: Do you think this case will go to trial?

LAWYER: They will want to settle because there is no way they can win on the facts. The evidence we have is overwhelming. You are going to be the face of the case.

POWERS: I'll do what I can to help.

LAWYER: We are going to give it our best shot. We have hearing set to go before members of the U.S.

Senate Judiciary Committee. We even built a mock cell that can be assembled right there at the hearing. We have the best experts in the world ready to give their testimony. If you were not such a maximum-security prisoner, we would get you there to testify.

POWERS: The administration will surely retaliate against me, but I don't care. What can they do to me? Put me in solitary confinement and torture me?

What is needed is a comprehensive overhaul of the federal criminal code. Everything needs to be erased, and the entire code needs to be replaced. I know this will never happen. As it stands now, the criminal justice system is in shambles. The law has become so complicated that nobody knows how to interpret it. Each district is its own kingdom with its own hierarchy. The application of the law is disparate and piecemeal. The punishments in many case are disproportionate and even draconian. The expense is astronomical. Those who are placed in prisons and jails are coming out worse than they were when they went in. The criminal justice system in America is not making society safer; it is making it more dangerous. But it is far too big and too involved to be effectively modified.

Solitary Confinement

KEEPING prisoners in solitary confinement is expedient for prison administrators. They have less to do to maintain control over the activities and behaviors of prisoners. I am locked inside an impenetrable concrete and steel box for 23 hours per day. I am allowed to go to another impenetrable concrete and steel box each day for recreation. The guards do their rounds, deliver food trays hand out mail, and supply cleaning supplies. The administrators do not have to deal with or even come into contact with me or any other prisoner here. It makes their jobs easier and ensures their safety. They claim it requires more funds to keep prisoners locked down, so they come out ahead on that end as well.

Their argument is that some prisoners are too dangerous to be placed in any setting other than solitary confinement. This may be true in some cases, but it is not true in all cases, and it is not true in my case. There are numerous prisoners in this place who do not truly need to be here. It is harmful to the prisoner. Long periods of solitary confinement can easily induce mental abnormalities. This much should be obvious to anybody who knows anything about human beings. In addition, prisoners often develop paranoia, they begin to have compulsive thoughts and behavior, they become lethargic. They can suddenly explode with anger. They eat, work out, or masturbate excessively. They do not want to leave solitary confinement. They may even become delusional or begin to hear voices.

The absence of human contact and normal sensory stimulation means there is something essential to good mental health that is missing. There is no point of reference. Many prisoners do reach a point where they begin to become unglued. This used to be called going stir crazy, and it is a real thing. Any pre-existing physical health issues can be impacted as well. Whether the extreme conditions are real or perceived makes no difference as to the result. Human beings are not adaptable to certain conditions, and one of those is solitary confinement. Prison officials readily admit that the purpose of these placements is to incapacitate the prisoner, and they know what they are talking about.

> LAWYER: Historically, it has always been the federal courts that have stepped up to remedy civil rights violations. But the courts cannot manage the day-to- day operations inside of a prison. We are fortunate to have a judge who is interested in this cause.

POWERS: But the hand off thing seems to slam the door on prisoners who desperately need relief. As you know, we don't have a lot of voice in matters that concern us.

LAWYER: It is difficult to get a court to listen, but we feel that this judge will listen. As you know, prisoners tend to abuse the legal system by filing frivolous complaints. This destroys their credibility and makes judges jaded. Then when someone comes along with a good claim, they tend to be ignored.

POWERS: What about all the frivolous litigation filed by attorneys?

LAWYER: You're right. But prisoners are probably less popular than lawyers. A lot of people think, "Let them rot in hell." But my firm has taken the position that prisoners who have mental illness must be treated for their mental illnesses, and we have come into the picture to represent those who are unable to be heard otherwise.

POWERS: You have really spent a lot of time and effort on this, and I appreciate it.

LAWYER: We still have a long way to go, and we are going to keep pressing forward.

It seems that those who are kept in solitude would be provided with positive activities. It cannot be too heavy of a lift to establish a comprehensive personal growth and development program for prisoners who are in solitary confinement. There also needs to be access to psychological services, when and if needed. The main idea should be to get the prisoner prepared to return to a general population as soon as possible. This falls under the auspices of reform-type programming, in other words, corrections. This involves influencing thoughts, feelings, and behavior in prosocial ways.

My head is like a merry-go-round. There is a lot of centrifugal force going on in my brain. I have times when I am involved with creative activities such as writing, drawing, and inventing. But then I have a persistent depression, anxiety, and dread that comes over me. I often wonder why I cannot contemplate a future for myself. There must be something in the cosmic mix that is haunting me or at least shadowing me. I feel that I need to bleed in order to feel alive again. It is an ugliness, I know, but I need to see it and feel it so I can get past it. The struggle that is in me keeps going around and around and does not stop.

It is evening and the sun is just going down. I have been feeling down and out again. I have made what looks like a chisel. It is a razor blade that is melted into a piece of a toothbrush that is flat on the top. I am going to use it to sever the achilles tendon on my ankle. I am not sure why I want to do this because it does not seem like a good idea... but I have it in my mind now, and there is only one way to get it out. So I position my leg on the edge of the concrete bunk and hold the chisel blade with one hand while I strike the top of it with the binding of a dictionary. The pain is both sharp and excruciating. It is at the top of the pain chart! I cannot even walk now.

When any person has been systematically depleted of his or her humanity, it is all but impossible to become whole again. That person will always feel that there is something missing, and that feeling cannot be easily shaken off. It seems to drag the person down like a weight perhaps like a ball-and-chain around an ankle. Mainly, it demands blood and pain and maybe something else. It is not exactly a sinister element, but it does dwell in the depths of the human psyche, and I believe it is in all of us. Normally it lies dormant, but once it is set loose, it cannot be made dormant again. It continues
to collect its tolls. It is the result of being kept in solitary confinement for too long.

PHYSICIAN: Why do you do these things to yourself? This is a serious injury. You could be crippled for life and unable to walk

POWERS: It doesn't matter. I don't have to walk that far anyway.

PHYSICIAN: But why did you do it? You must have had a reason.

POWERS: Stress relief.

PHYSICIAN: There are better ways to relieve your stress. Have you tried yoga?

POWERS: Yes, in fact, I have.

I get the sense that there is not much difference between cops and criminals. It is clear to me that the staff here lies and manipulates as much if not more than the prisoners. It is also clear to me that staff can be dangerous. There is a good deal of incompetence and error. In some instances, this has meant the difference between life and death for someone. It is easier for staff to ignore problems that are too complicated or burdensome for them. I want to be fair to everyone, but it is exceedingly difficult not to be biased. My own experience is that staff only responds to those who are belligerent, disruptive, or completely out of control. When someone is genuinely trying to do the right thing, he is bound to get screwed over every time.

> *I returned from a visit with the lawyer to find my cell trashed and torn up. It does not make me mad any longer: maybe for a hot minute, and then I am over it. I have to learn how to maintain my own state of mind and not be unduly reactive. Worse is to allow another person or persons to dictate the way I feel about myself and my life. So, I simply take it in stride and go about the process of cleaning up. I am going to do what I do, and they are going to do what they do. It is that simple.*

Beginning to Heal

THE achilles tendon is healing back together nicely. They had to perform surgery in order to reconnect it. I was in a cast and was supposed to wear it for eight weeks, but I took it off after a week or so. The reason I took it off was so that I could put my foot and ankle in the sink and soak it in hot water. The water temperature gets pretty hot probably 150 degrees, and it cooks my foot and ankle like a lobster! I start out with water I can stand and keep increasing the temperature until it is as high as it can go. This cooking is working. I can already walk on it a little bit.

> *My friend and I are on the teeter-totter at school. We sometimes hold the other person in the up position. My friend holds me up in the air by keeping his weight on the very end of the board. For whatever reason, I decide to show off by hanging upside down, but he jumps off his side of the board and I crash into the ground at an odd angle. When I get up, something is wrong. I cannot move my right arm. I ride my bicycle around the neighborhood one-handed until it is time for supper. At the table, my mother notices that I am hurt, and she takes me to the emergency room at a local hospital. The doctor applies some kind of a wrap that goes around both shoulders and meets up in the back. It is coated with some kind of plaster that dries as hard as a rock. I have to wear this contraption for what seems like forever.*

People have asked me if I believe in "God." The answer depends on their definition of God. I do not believe in some supernatural human-like old man with a white beard who lives up on a cloud. That sounds too much like Santa Claus to me, and there is no evidence that supports it. To me, God is the concept of a kind of goodness that is not typically human. This energy or element is most likely the source of intelligence, compassion, and hope. What people refer to as "God" means "Divine Goodness" to me. It makes more sense to me that way than the old man model.

I am striving to cultivate the qualities and skills of my mind that make for good and decent human beings. There are too many folks who are hung up on superstition. It is impossible for me to go along with it. Unfortunately, there are many whose beliefs about God, themselves, and the world around them are immature. These are readily identified because they cause conflict and hatred, and because of them a lot of hurt and harm is brought into this world. It is much too hard for me to figure out what all is going on in the universe. I have a hard enough time trying to figure out what is going on in my own heart and mind to me, God equals Divine Goodness, and that is what it boils down to. To follow God is to seek whatever goodness is within me.

This simple concept that God equals Good is how I began the personal training manual I am working on. By examining the words and actions of certain well-known historical figures, their characteristics can be identified. These can be categorized and given names like truthfulness, forgiveness, humility, service, perseverance, et cetera. I now have thirty that together, are representative of an enhanced human personality. The main idea is to create a process a method that is effective in inducing these qualities and skills into the depths of my psyche. I am trying to assemble a lot of information from a variety of sources and then break it all down to something simple, if possible. They are standards to strive for.

> *Human life is an ordeal for everyone. It is no easy thing 10 be born human, and the advent of civilization does not make it easier. In fact, it can all become rather complicated. Our natural impulses our instincts have to be curtailed or suppressed altogether. To feel good about ourselves we must need to accomplish something, hopefully something good. And what is good is simply whatever is not bad. It takes some effort to push ourselves beyond ordinary fears and desires, yet we do have that capability when we choose to use it. There is no way we can be good. We can only exert ourselves in the cause of what is good. When we reach for what is good, we feel good.*

There are seven ways I have discovered, by trial and error, that help me to feel good: (1) Thinking about what I am thankful for, (2) Making a list of what I want to accomplish for the day and moving toward those goals, (3) Catching myself whenever I begin to think negative thoughts and choosing to change them, (4) Realizing that there are going to be setbacks, (5) Taking advantage of every opportunity to better myself, (6) Staying away from those who are poor influences on my state of mind, and (7) Enjoying the accomplishments as they reveal themselves.

The problem is that I do not always stay within these guidelines. It is a struggle for me. I have been knifed, spit on, threatened, sucker-punched, choked unconscious, tormented, humiliated, tortured, starved, hated, taken advantage of you name it and it has had an effect on me. It is the kind of thing I have come to expect, or anticipate, and it makes me over-reactive emotionally. I know I should see it as a test on what I have learned, but I get caught up in the moment and forget what I thought I had learned. It is frustrating! There are so many people in the world who have it far worse than I do, and here I am feeling sorry for myself. It is like a fire that seems innocuous at a distance, but up close and personal is devastating.

All of this mess has taught me valuable lessons, but I know that I will also have to keep learning them over and over again. As long as I am alive I can heal. It is certainly a challenge. Just when I think I am beginning to heal, something else happens to tear that wound open again. Yet I feel I am on the right track. At least I am trying. Every day I am trying to become a better human being, and that is the best I can do. There is no way to erase the past and start over. It does not happen that way. I only have an opaque idea about how to follow the path of life that pursues the good, and it is often hard to stay on it.

> *Much of the wisdom of our ancient ancestors has been lost to time. But it is fortunate that this wisdom can be recovered by those who are heroic in their search for understanding. What can be understood may not be much, but it is better than nothing. Being able to quiet the movements of the body and the thought of the mind is essential. It is within this silence that wisdom grows. The breath is the focus, and it is the link to quietude. To sit still and to put the attention of the mind on the breath only is the method of expanding understanding that is common throughout human history. It is in the depths of silence that divine goodness can be approached.*

There is not much to do here except to think. I have no real need to think, but I do it a lot. There are few distractions, and I have come to consider thinking as being an art. The main idea is to stay focused on a central subject and work around the edges until the pieces begin to fall into place. I try to be objective, and I find that intelligence is less of an asset than practice. My cell is like a think tank. My mind amazes me because it has all kinds of hidden capabilities that must be uncovered. It is like a treasure hunt.

Things have been relatively quiet here. The lawyers come around to the visiting room every now and then. Overall, the staff has not changed much. Most likely, this legal effort will bring minimal changes. The lawyers want system-wide

policies and procedures, but it seems to me that there are other objectives that have nothing to do with prisoners. There is a giant, brand spanking new maximum-security prison that sits empty in the State of Illinois. The state built it but did not use it for some reason. The senator who held
the hearings on the ADX Supermax happens to represent that state, and he has been pushing for the U.S. government to purchase that prison as part of the remedy. There is nothing illegal about it; but there is a couple of hundred million dollars involved, and the ADX litigation creates leverage.

If anything good ever does come from the lawsuit here, it is most likely that it will accrue to people other than the prisoners. The lawyers keep on saying they are doing it pro bono, for free, but I cannot imagine they have no way to get paid. Lawyers always get paid. But they certainly have the right to operate as a business as far as I am concerned. I am hoping that the prisoners who have languished for many years in solitary confinement under the burdens of untreated mental illness can get paid something. Unfortunately, the Bureau of Prisons would rather compensate anyone other than prisoners; it is afraid of setting a precedent.

> *There is a tree growing in the corner of the outside area that I can see from my cell. It is growing between the cracks in the concrete way over in the corner. It has obviously been there for some time, but I never saw it before. It is wispy and elegant and beautiful. I am instantly in love with it. I stand with my head pressed at an odd angle and look at her for hours. I talk to her and tell her how lovely, how awesome, how brave she is to have come to such a place. But I am struck with a terrible fear that the staff will find out about her and chop her down. They will not allow her to reign with all her majesty in the midst of a concrete and steel no-man's land. They will not allow her to give us hope.*

The Death of Beauty

POWERS has been doing all right as of late. He has been calm and cool dealing with it. He is still confined in the control unit, but he now has the opportunity to make two 15-minute collect calls per month. This is what he looks forward to the most. He has another picture of Jesus that he keeps affixed to the outer shower wall. He sits on his folded blanket at night, burns a candle made from margarine oil, and talks to Jesus. He has a TV set that gets satellite music channels, and he has found a way to use the long ear bud wires to hook up to the speaker in the intercom. He also has some sandalwood incense sticks that the former prisoner left in the cell when he moved.

> *There is a lot of sadness. It is all over the place. What a plight we humans have as we trudge along the course of our lives. We try to put a good face on it, but the underlying realities are like rocks in our shoes. People probably gravitate toward sex and drugs and music in an effort to get their minds free for a time. They can hardly be blamed. What we are trying to avoid is the fact that we are all walking around every day with a sword poised over our necks. The knowledge of impending death is the great sadness that everyone carries around and cannot get rid of. It causes a lot of distress. We turn on one another because of it.*

It is a Sunday afternoon and Powers has a telephone call scheduled. He has to press the duress button several times
to remind the guards on duty to bring the phone. They finally come onto the range, open the out-cell door, and push the phone into the sally port. They tell Powers to check to make sure it is working before they leave. The phone is a black steel contraption that stands about 4 foot high and has an old-style handset and buttons that sound a tone when pressed. Powers thanks them and hurries to punch in the number he is calling. After several rings, his mother answers and accepts the call.

POWERS: Hi, mom. How's everything?

MOM: Well, not too good. Your sister is in the hospital and is not in good shape. We are trusting the Lord to heal her.

POWERS: What? What's wrong with her?

MOM: Something with her liver. They thinks it's cancer there and she may need a transplant.

POWERS: How does that work? Is there a donor?
MOM: Well, I don't know how that works. We have to go back up to the hospital as soon as I'm off the phone with you. We only came home to freshen up and have a rest. We were up there all last night.

POWERS: She can have mine; you know. We are probably a match since we are brother and sister. I know that Bureau of Prisons' policy does allow for prisoners to donate their organs.

MOM: Well, we don't know what they will end up doing. She is in intensive care right now, and they have her hooked into all kinds of machines.

POWERS: Let them know that they have a potential donor over here. I have no diseases, no Hep-C, no nothing wrong with my blood.

Powers is extremely affected by this news. He walks back and forth, back and forth, for hours. He refuses the food trays when they come, and he is thinking. He is trying to figure out what is going on and how he can help. He is thinking about his sister and how beautiful and kind she is, but he also thinks that she has delayed treatment because of her faith. The church that she, her husband and daughter attend believes in faith healing, and it is likely that they were exercising their faith until she got so sick she could not continue without medical intervention. Powers is twisting and turning everything in his mind. He thinks that this could be exactly what he has been wanting a chance for him to give something back to his family.

The next day, Powers tries to get information about what he must do in order to donate his liver to his sister. He stops the PA when he comes on the range to deliver medications to the others and inquires. He learns important things: yes, he can donate a portion of his liver because the liver is the only organ that can regenerate itself. The PA tells Powers that there are a lot of procedures and protocols to go through before anything can be done. The insurance company would

need to contact the Bureau of Prisons to arrange testing and payment because the Bureau would not pay for any of it. To
Powers, this all sounds doable, and he is buoyed by the prospects. More than anything else in his life he wants to give his sister his liver, or whatever part of she needs.

Now, Powers needs to make another phone call. The problem is that he has already made his two for the month. He begs and pleads with any and every staff member that comes onto the range all to no avail. They tell him that it is not an emergency phone call because no one has died, and he tells them that his sister may very well die if he cannot relay information to his family. This is not enough to convince them. They say if they do it for Powers, they will have to do it for every other inmate. They tell Powers to write a letter and put everything in that. Powers protests and says that it might take a couple of weeks for a letter to get to his family. They indicate that it is all that can be done.

> *Powers is beside himself with anger and frustration. He cannot believe the circumstances. He has written several letters and given them to the guards for placement in the mail. He can only keep hoping that they get there. It is maddening! Why are medical staff not coming to take the blood needed for the testing? Why is nobody on top of this? Powers wants to cut out his own liver, if need be, and send it in a box of dry ice. He has been pacing back and forth so much, he has worn holes in his socks. He is in so much emotional pain; he has to stop and kneel down and cry every so often. He keeps washing the tears off of his face because he does not want the guards to know how much he has been crying.*

Those days were the absolute hardest days to deal with. To be on such an intense emotional roller coaster for days in and days out begins to take a toll. There is no way to describe it with mere words. Even the attempt to do so can only be pathetic. Some few days later the chaplain and the captain came onto the range and had control open Powers' outer door. They were somber as they stepped inside the sally port. The chaplain told Powers that they had been informed that Powers' sister had died. They said they were sorry to hear it and that Powers was allowed to make one phone call.

The beautiful tree in the corner outside is gone. I saw the facilities people going around with weed whackers and other landscaping tools on a cart. I was hoping so much so utterly desperately that they would leave the tree alone. They had to know how vitally important that tree had been to the men here who could see it. To cut it down was an act of cruelty that exceeded all others. These people who call themselves good and decent men because they keep people inside cages and, thereby, protect the public from them are heartless and cruel in ways those in the cages never dreamed of.

Powers stands at the mirror on the wall, looking at his face. He notices once again how much he has aged. He touches around his eyes and tries to see into them. He wonders about
who he is and what his life means. He has a razor in his hand, and he holds it up in front of the mirror. He touches his earlobes and pulls on them, one and the other. Then he cuts them off. He also cuts long incisions down each side of his face in front of his ears. The blood pours out and is all over both him and the floor within seconds. The blood has a familiar warmth and makes a distinctive sound when it hits the floor.

> *It is getting dark, and we are still playing kickball out in the backyard. It is one of those evenings during summer vacation where neighborhood kids get together to play some kind of a game. There are mosquitoes out, and a few fireflies flashing around. Someone kicks the ball, and it goes way out by the pine trees. I have to chase it down. Just beyond the pines I see my sister sitting on the ground with one of the older neighborhood boys. They are sort of looking at the sky and probably feeling like they might be in love. I run back and throw the ball, but the runner has already cleared the bases and is home.*

Winds of Change

THERE are changes coming. Those who hold high positions are beginning to restructure certain elements of the criminal justice system. This will, of necessity, be incremental. Nobody will be put out of work or prejudiced. In fact, the changes will bring many new benefits to everyone concerned. At present, the federal penitentiaries are out of control. There is far too much murder and mayhem going on inside of them. Prisoners have long sentences, no valid programming to speak of, and not much incentive to stay out of trouble. With the advent of new and modern synthetic drugs, the general populations are cauldrons of violence, rage, and racism. There are so many gangs now that new prisoners are forced to join up.

As mentioned, one of the biggest problems is institutionalization. This is a long word for a person who cannot adapt to life in society. As a result, that person must be housed and cared for in every way for the remainder of his or her natural life. There is some element of survival that rules human biology that follows the path of least resistance. These unconscious impulses always make the mind act against reason, and they usually involve either staying in prison or going back to prison, take your pick. It is a strange and powerful phenomenon of the psyche that has the most debilitating effect on prisoners. In his or her conscious mind, the prisoner is saying, "When I get out I am never coming back to this hellhole again!" But the unconscious is saying, "Let's go back to the place where we had a roof over our head, food to eat, clothing, medical care and everything else supplied free of charge."

In this sense, prison itself may very well be the root cause of crime, compulsions, and addictive behavior. In the future, it is most likely that new technologies and methods will be used to help train better qualities and skills into the personality. Schools will not focus of academics as a priority, but on inculcating good character and effective people skills. Indeed, personal growth and development is going to become the main theme in mainstream American society. Those who are involved with drugs, gangs, and criminal activities will reformulate their organizations and mindsets. They will begin to change their ways and work to become assets to their communities as opposed to liabilities.

The leaders in every community will invest their time, interests, energy, knowledge, and money into altering the path of at-risk youngsters. This is not guesswork; this is a necessity. The emphasis will be placed on social adjustment, crime prevention, and meaningful participation. No one will be ignored or left out. Children will be trained in good character at the earliest ages possible, and the training will be evidence-based. Their progress will be monitored, and interventions applied if needed. Parents will begin to spend more time with their kids and will be examples for them. The corporations will become more and more responsible for what is happening in the communities they do business with. The politicians will guide the processes of law so that they produce the results intended. Everyone will find a new sense of themselves, a new sense of community, and a new sense of country.

The number one priority for the criminal justice system ought to be the elimination or reduction of violent crime. To
do this, violent crimes must be well defined and separate from all other crimes and offenses. There must be zero tolerance for serious violent crime, and this must be coordinated across both state and federal jurisdictions. Every other kind of crime would be easier to deal with if violence was isolated. One of the reasons there are so many criminals is that there are so many laws that make so many acts criminal. There certainly needs to be law and order, but it needs to be rational. The paradigm of crime and punishment must be changed to the extent that it reflects its main goal: correction of poor behavior in society.

> LAWYER: Good to see you again. What is this, the eleventh or twelfth time we have visited you?

> POWERS: It's been quite a few.

> LAWYER: We now have a panel of experts who are second to none, and I expect to file an amended complaint and ask for class action certification.

> POWERS: Do you think any permanent good will come from this.

> LAWYER: It will. This is going to be a case that will set the tone for prison litigation throughout the entire country. This is a pretty big deal.

> POWERS: How is the Vega case going?

> LAWYER: We are in the Tenth Circuit on appeal, but we should win it.

> POWERS: How can you lose?

> LAWYER: These things are complicated...But how are you doing?

POWERS: I endure. I don't know how all of this is going to turn out, but I will hang in there and try to support the effort the best I can.

LAWYER: Good deal.

It is true that I need to figure out what to do. I do have a direct interest in pursuing whatever legal relief can be obtained. Things are beginning to change here. They brought in several new psychologists, they are implementing new policies and procedures, and they are looking at creating special programs for prisoners who have mental illness. Because I have mutilated myself and am involved in the lawsuit, the Bureau of Prisons will probably send me out of here. The only thing I can hope for is that I do not end up back in that shithole they call Springfield.

The administration has decided to move me out of the control unit and onto what they call a general population range. It is not all that much different than the control unit. We do get an additional phone call each month, and we do get to go outside for more hours each day. When I went outside, a whole flock of sparrows came and landed on the fencing all around me. They were chattering and carrying on like we were all old friends. They were somehow drawn to the pattern of my tattoos, I think, but they may have sensed my spirit and understood that I am their friend. From now on I will smuggle bread and rice and other things they like to eat to them when I go outside.

There have been dozens of media reports now: magazines, newscasts, documentaries, and radio. Hearings in Washington, international coverage, and even a U.N. committee have come into play. Many of these use a picture of me in my meditation posture. I have been busy with all the correspondence, thinking and writing, and meeting with the lawyers and experts. Somehow the pieces have begun to come together. Mostly everyone agrees that there is a significant problem, and that something constructive needs to be done about it. I am glad about it, but I am too jaded to be exhilarated.

My main project is what I am now calling THE MANUAL Program. It is a set of thirty instructions one for each day of the average month. I do a number of deep breathing exercises to clear my mind before reading the day's instruction. I am constantly experimenting, adjusting, rewriting and trying to make it more comprehensive and effective. The main problem is that it is too lengthy. Each instruction is four or five pages long. This is not too long for me, but I think it might be for others. I am trying to develop a system that works toward influencing the deeper mind in terms of how it process thought, feelings, and action. Studies show that somewhere around 80 percent of families are dysfunctional. This means that we do not know how to act. And although we may not resort to criminal behavior per se, there are far too many of us who are otherwise off the rails. Consider all of the addictions; consider all of the secret and not-so-secret abuses; consider all of the bad acts that are not technically violations of the law. In my view there is a compelling need for a curriculum that actually changes the way a person thinks, feels, and acts. There are indeed standards of human behavior that must be pursued. These standards depend on influencing the way a person processes information.

The long-standing theory on prisoners is that they are born to be criminals and that there is no way to alter their behavior. This is the central premise of the expansion of the prison industrial complex. But this is a lazy way of thinking. It is true that in many instances a particular prisoner may seem to be outside the scope of rehabilitation, but that prisoner can be influenced in prosocial and positive ways. Maybe later on it is the difference between that person shooting someone in the head or letting them go. It is difficult, perhaps, to make these distinctions at the outset, but the possibilities should not be foreclosed.

There are a lot of men and women who are sitting in cages at this moment who have nothing but time on their hands. At least some of them want to turn their lives around. They are sick and tired of being sick and tired. They see that there

is nothing good that is happening for them in their current circumstances. Yet they do not know what to do in order to transform the trajectory of their lives. The thing about educational opportunities is all well and good, but this is not the premiere initiative needed. If the characteristics of the personality are not effectively enhanced, the education of a criminal only produces a smarter criminal.

It is the early morning hours here. The cell is cold, and it is snowing lightly outside. I am up, walking and talking, and trying to figure things out. It is peaceful now. Earlier today there was another suicide. One of the new-line psychologists told me about it. The guards brought around a good meal afterwards and were quite courteous and helpful to everyone. The director of the bureau of prisons has been called to give testimony before the judicial committee. There is also a draft policy about psychological treatment programs being floated around. Even the president has made statements about the issues involved in our litigation. Yet I remain skeptical about all of it. In a way, I am pleased that something is happening, but there is always a dread that lurks in the background of my mind. In any case, right now I am walking around in two pairs of socks and sipping my coffee and not worrying about it too much.

The Suicide Club

ALL of my friends are dead. Well, not quite all of them, but quite a few of them are. Many of those who I tried to befriend made later decisions to end their own lives, and some were killed by others. It is a strange initiation into a strange club. One prisoner who was next to me and hated my guts kept on telling me to kill myself. He himself ended up committing suicide only a few weeks ago. The most recent one was only a glance from a young man who was walking across the unit in handcuffs and shackles. He looked at me as if to say, "Watch me go." The next day I did watch as they removed his lifeless body from his cell.

Throughout my years in solitary confinement, the notions of suicide stalked me. As I look back, it seems like every time I really wanted to go for it someone else stepped up to take my place. I am getting to where I am afraid to talk to other prisoners for fear they will get caught up in whatever other worldly phenomena is going on and kill themselves. I have stated many times that I have no problem with anyone committing suicide if they have no hope whatsoever for a better future and are already miserable. I also believe that suicide is the ultimate form of protest for prisoners who are truly under the gun, trapped in a pocket of torment, and have no viable means of ever getting out.

It is all too true that I am not the most optimistic person to be around. Throw in a shitty dinner tray or bad news from the courts and I can be downright negative. I have a knack for crushing false hope when the facts do not support it. The realities of human life as I understand them do not make me
want to wish them away. My life has been my life, and I am not ashamed of it. Sure, I could have done a lot better, but the reality is that I did what I did, and now I have to own it. If there ever is a next time, I will do much better now that I know what I did not know before.

Criminal thinking has been outside of my wheelhouse since Eddie was murdered. I understood, right off the bat, that my internal status and identity had taken a dramatic turn. I wanted to get as far away from those who operate under criminal minds as I could. Maybe the solitary confinement was helpful to me in that regard. It certainly kept me out of circulation for a good number of years. Now, with the advent of the ADX litigation, the bureau of prisons has agreed to modify existing housing units at several of its penitentiaries to create independent psychological treatment programs. these are supposed to have the same basic features that I have been advocating for: that is, personal growth and development curriculums, individualized treatment plans, and incentives. It is satisfying to see that I have been an instrumental part of something like this.

Any person who spends 23 hours a day stuffed inside a cage about the size of a small bathroom might just think about suicide. It seems like that would be a logical thought particularly when other debilitating factors are present. It is not inevitable by any means, but it seems natural. Hell, I wish someone could tell me how to live in a cage and be happy about it! Some of my fellow captives seem to know the secret. They run around giggling and haw hawing and act like they love it here. I do not know how they do it. They say that you just have to accept it, but I cannot accept it. It always feels wrong to me, and I do not want it to feel right.

LAWYER: Everything is going our way. The judge has ruled in our favor on several key points. We are going to keep pressing for a settlement.

POWERS: But isn't the point of the whole thing to raise public awareness? If you settle, the B.O.P. gets off lightly like a plea bargain.

LAWYER: That's right. But I am confident we can get more in a settlement than we can get at a trial.

POWERS: Will there be any compensation for any of the plaintiffs?

LAWYER: Probably not. The B.O.P. will not allow it, and they are adamant about that. So, we are looking for injunctive relief, which means the judge will order the B.O.P. to do certain things and will monitor them to make sure they do them.

POWERS: It's not anything remedial, then, for the named plaintiffs? We won't get damages.

LAWYER: That's right. We can't do much about what happened in the past, but we can make sure that other prisoners do not have to go through what you have had to go through. This case was never about money.

POWERS: I am quite sure that you and your firm are going to get paid, and I have nothing against that. But there are prisoners who were seriously abused who should get something.

LAWYER: We are not going that route. The B.O.P. will never agree to give any one of you one red cent.

POWERS: They will be able to deny liability?

LAWYER: Yes, but that is a technicality.

POWERS: A technicality?

It is all semantics. It is like when the health services people came to me and wanted me to sign all kinds of forms. They wanted to know where to send my personal things, who to contact, what medical procedures I was willing to forego. They wanted to know who would make arrangements for the disposal of my body. I talked with them and signed their papers. They were trying to cover their asses, of course. My mortality is an ever-present reality. I live with thoughts of death every day because I have chronic PTSD and that is part of its effect. There is always a force that pushes in that direction, and the medical experts are very much aware of it.

There are many prisoners who have undiagnosed PTSD. If they had contracted it as members of the military, they would be properly diagnosed and treated. But since they happen to be lowly, scum of the earth criminals in the minds of prison rats, they have nothing coming. This is a terrible offense against humanity. To force people to suffer an affliction up to and including the point of suicide is itself a crime. I reject all of it as being pure nonsense. There is absolutely no question that prison staff manipulate the mental health diagnoses of prisoners to suit the administrations' needs, not the prisoner's.

Here I go thinking I am somebody. The truth is, I am nobody. There is nothing special about me. I did not even graduate high school. The list of my accomplishments could be written on a postage stamp. I have been a sorry criminal and pot head for most of my life, and I have spent the majority of my adult life inside prisons and jails from one end of the country to the other. Why should I become angry when people treat me poorly? To think of myself or to present myself as some kind of

115

a crusader for justice is absurd. The only thing I really know is prison and crime and security and punishment and death. Where do I come up with the temerity to posture and pose and think I am somebody?

Human life is such a mystery. Everyone is alone, but we are all alone together. We want to move onward, but we seem to find ourselves stuck in a conundrum of circumstance. We very much want to live, yet we temp death at every turn. Our bodies grow old and get worn out while we are still trying to figure out what life is all about. I have never been able to understand why people are so afraid, so dumb...We are all going to die, you know. Our bodies and minds commit suicide! If a person puts himself in harm's way and ends up dead, it can be argued that he committed suicide. I find that we continue to operate on other people's notions while failing to determine our own, and we suffer as a result.

They are coming to get me in a few minutes. The lieutenant on duty came and said that I will be going down to R&D before breakfast. He told me to pack up my things and to be ready when they come for me. So, these are my last moments here in this place where I have lived for many years. I am looking around and trying to capture how I feel about this sudden news. I suppose I should be glad, but in fact it seems that I am actually sad. So much of my life has been spent here, so much of my blood has been spilled here, and so many of my dreams have come and gone here. I have no idea of where I am being transferred to. I am hoping it is one of the new treatment units, but who knows. No one will tell me where I am going, and I will not be able to figure it out until I get there. It is all right. I was not doing much anyway, and it is as good a day as any for a field trip.

Some years ago I was writing to a lady whose daughter was dying from an aggressive form of bone cancer. I suggested that the daughter face the reality of her situation, make the most of her remaining time, and pull the plug in a dignified way. That lady never wrote to me again. Her daughter, from what I heard, had a traumatic and terrible death that put her loved ones through hell. It seems like those who are already on death's doorstep would have no objection to a quick and painless exit, but some of them want to hang on to the bitter end. Conversely, it seems that a person who has a lot to live for would be less likely to commit suicide, but this is not so in every case either.

116

The Law Speaks

WE drew the Judge who presided over the Oklahoma City Bombing case. He is a strict law and order judge, but he also has a reputation for being fair and honest. The attorney for the government is a tough litigator who also happens to be a decent human being. The new Warden at the ADX is an upright sort who also believes that remedial action is necessary. In fact, there is no real opposition to the ADX lawsuit. The Bureau of Prisons has opened its files and records to the lawyers, and the lawyers are taking full advantage. They are logging all of the hours possible. The work that is happening is like a whirlwind of paperwork. No one is going to be held personally responsible.

Typically, it is not easy to win a lawsuit against the federal government. Federal judges are not some unbiased jurists that are selected from the general bar; they are specifically recommended by senators and the U.S. Justice Department and are appointed by the president. They are not people who are readily going to go against the grain. And the people who surround the federal judges marshals, clerks, secretaries, legal assistants and others are like part of a big family. In other words, they all know each other, and they all have roles to play as a team. Together, they wield a lot of power over the matters that come before them. They are known to given prisoners short shrift.

Prisoners have a hard time getting any federal court to rule in their favor particularly on conditions of confinement cases. Any prisoner who is brave enough to try is forced to jump through hoops like circus dogs. They have to use the proper forms, pay the full filing fees, past preliminary screenings, and follow all of the rules and orders of the court to the letter. And this is all before any defendant has even been served. Prisoners who are filing a civil rights complaint against prison officials are really up against it. They are locked in cages and have little or no access to evidence or information supporting their claims. They must rely on the very people they are suing for copies, postage, delivery of mail, and access to legal materials.

There is the ever-present problem of credibility. Where other litigants can make statements and representations to a court that are taken as true, prisoners do not have that luxury. The main reason is that prisoners are indeed prone to make things up, or to overstate or exaggerate the facts, or to falsify evidence. The thought is that they have nothing to lose anyway. Some prisoners become "frequent fliers" in the court system by filing a plethora of frivolous complaints many of them demanding millions in damages. The courts get used to dismissing prisoner complaints on that basis alone. Therefore, it is a minor miracle when a prisoner actually wins any kind of relief from the federal courts. Suffice it to say that it is not normal for prisoners to catch the ear of a judge.

Many of the amendments to the U.S. Constitution deal with the rights of those accused of crimes. The law surrounding these rights is spotty at best. It is very complex and somewhat pathetic. When the government is hit with a lawsuit there are all kinds of defenses available: failure to exhaust administrative remedies, qualified immunity, failure to state a claim, procedural violations, and summary judgment are among them. The elements that a prisoner must prove are hard for even trained attorneys with all kinds of resources to understand. No individual staff member can be held personally liable if he or she was on the job when the alleged violation occurred. There are so many layers of protection that to penetrate them all requires an Act of God.

> POWERS: So what you are wanting to do is to get the Bureau of Prisons to do what it should have been doing all along. Do I have that right?

> LAWYER: We want to force the B.O.P. to develop new policies regarding psychological services at the ADX and elsewhere, including the control unit.

> POWERS: How is it that the B.O.P. never had or followed these requirements in the first place? Doesn't the Eighth Amendment prohibit cruel and unusual punishment?

> LAWYER: Yes, that's right.

> POWERS: I don't think a court is going to be able to solve the problem. I think it has to be done by the Congress.

> LAWYER: I am going to have to disagree. A court order will be faster, and it will apply nationwide. Legislation is too speculative. Here, we have a sure thing. The B.O.P cannot win on the facts or law in this case, and everyone knows it.

Unfortunately, once any governmental system is up and running it is nearly impossible to alter its core operations. The institution itself becomes institutionalized. It is habit, routine, the path of least resistance. Even the administrators know that there is an inertia involved that is going to require a lot of motivation to overcome. No one seems to have any idea about how long it will take to sort everything out. It could be years. I do know that the other named prisoner plaintiffs do not want to settle for policy changes. They want a public trial and a chance to tell their stories. They also want a compensation fund set up so they can recover at least some compensatory damages.

> *The consensus by lawyers, judges, politicians, career administrators, and reporters is that prisoners in the United States must be able to receive adequate treatment for mental health issues. To deny this treatment is the equivalent of cruel and unusual punishment. moreover, the practice of sending men or women or juveniles into solitary confinement for lengthy periods of time also constitutes cruel and unusual punishment. These are excesses of punishment that cause more harm than good. The focus on treatment will, over time, produce much better results than the current approach.*

It is hard for Powers to keep on reliving everything that has happened especially the deaths of his friends and family. It seems to him that the event of his life keep going around in a big circle but, at the same time, are moving forward. Even though his own circumstances may not change all that much, it is possible that things could change for other prisoners. The main part of it is the control unit policies. In the future, prisoners who have serious mental illness will not be placed in the control unit. They may not be placed at the ADX at all. This means that young men like Gato will be able to get the help they need to keep on living.

> *They told me about the big horse. they said not to take him out to ride because he would buck me off and run back to the barn. Me being me, I took him out anyway. We were doing so good. He plodded along the trail with his head in rhythm with his shoulders. I figured if he was going to break bad, he would have done it before we got too far away from the barn. I was lulled into a sense of security. I patted him on the neck and called him a good horse and his ears perked up as if he understood. Then he turned to the side and threw his hips into the air, and I went flying into the air and landed in the weeds. Meanwhile, the horse took off at a high rate of speed, running for the barn and, presumably, the hay that was in his feeder. it was a long walk back, and I had plenty of time to cuss him out.*

At least I have a powerful organization standing with me in my battle against the machine. It seems an improbable

scenario that such things could happen. It went from me being alone and being effectively incapacitated even emasculated to me having the assistance of one of the biggest and most prestigious law firms in the world.

Recently I told the lawyers that if there was going to be a trial, that I wanted to testify last. They assured me that they would arrange it if it came to that. On the other hand, they keep on talking about settlement. The plaintiffs want three things: (1) the opportunity to tell their stories in a public forum, (2) a compensation fund, and (3) monitoring of any settlement agreement for an extended period of time.

Imagine It

IMAGINE being forcefully separated from the people you love and from your home and community. Imagine being physically assaulted and put into chains and taken away to a cage. Imagine spending years under lock and key in solitary confinement. Imagine the boredom, the depression, and the despair that must be endured. Imagine being forced to rely on your captors for every item or activity that is a part of life in the cage. Imagine being constantly watched, constantly suspected of some misbehavior. Imagine being alone and left without any source of help or comfort, surrounded by those who are under the same conditions, and deprived of life's normal experiences. Imagine the hatred and violence and fear that is pervasive throughout the entire environment. How is any of this going to be helpful?

Powers has likely been damaged far more than he knows. Yet, he has also been regenerated. The way he thinks about himself, and his life has changed dramatically. There are things that have been taken from him that cannot be replaced, but what those are is hard for him to enumerate. Some days find him filled with optimism, and other days find him in the depths of despair. The way he feels is different now. A lot of the things he thought to be important have turned out to be unimportant. He has a different set of problems now and none of them are problems he can solve by himself. He needs to connect on some meaningful level with others who need to connect on some meaningful level. He is at a bit of a loss because he cannot see the way out.

> *Something is going on here and I do not know what it is.*
> *Whatever it is moves within both the noise and the silence. It is*
> *in the chilly air, the flush of a toilet, the words on a page. It is a*
> *mystery that is a part of everything, everywhere. it is a giant*
> *question mark that hangs in the air and waits for someone to*
> *notice. When it does speak, its language is beyond what is*
> *comprehensible. It is old, so very old, that not even the sky can*
> *comprehend it. The mystery of the ages. it has always been and*
> *will always be.*

Living inside a cage is too far beyond what I am convinced is right. There is nothing rational about depleting a person's body and mind in a place like this. Years ago I was sitting in a holding cell full of prisoners. One of them was all smiles even after having just received a stiff sentence. So I asked him how he could still be happy. He said, "My only other choice is to go around being

122

miserable all the time." That bit of logic has stuck with me over the years, though I find it hard to employ. I am no longer miserable, but neither am I happy. There has been some kind of a balance reached an equilibrium of sorts that I can work with.

Imagine having to wake up every day, trapped within the same cage, suffocated by the same dire circumstances. There is some-thing dark that has gnawed a hole in Powers' heart and is working on his mind. It is biting off chunks of his humanity and is spitting them into his face. Every day is the same old ugliness, the same drab existence, the same tired discouragement. He does have the choice whether to continue or not. It is not that he cannot take it because he has proven time and again that he can but more like why keep putting up with it. The one thing that keeps him going is his new mission in life, for he had an epiphany.

> *Human life is not an easy thing for anybody. It may be easier for some than for others, but no one gets out of it unscathed. There is always stress and pain and heartbreak. People struggle to find meaning, acceptance and joy. It always seems that there is something better up ahead, but it is hard to grasp. Sometimes it is difficult to know what the right thing is to do and sometimes it is even more difficult to do it. There seems to be confusion and, at times, distress. There are many of us who suffer quietly behind the scenes. We have become good at it.*

As a result of the ADX litigation, things that were impossible on a while ago are now possible. Powers has met a good number of very decent human beings, and they have each in their own way given him an intangible gift. He sincerely appreciates each and every one of them together with all their efforts on his behalf. He hopes to one day be released from prison, and he intends to pass along their kindness and goodness to others who need it as much as he has. There is no way that Powers can still owe any debt whatsoever to society because society has collected in full, and then some. However, he still feels that he owes it to himself and to those who believed in him to do something meaningful with his life what is left of it.

> LAWYER: Everything is going our way. The judge has ruled in our favor again. We are going to settle.

> POWERS: If you think it is best to settle, I have no objections. As long as the primary plaintiffs get something, I will go along with it.

LAWYER: They are not going to authorize a compensation fund, and everyone's statement to the court will have to be done on video. There is no way to get everyone up to the courthouse.

POWERS: But can't you use a portion of the attorneys' fees to set up a compensation fund? That's what you said you would do during the settlement conference in the ADX gymnasium.

LAWYER: We can't do that. We are going to give a million to a Denver University that has a law clinic, and we are going to give another million to the Washington Lawyer's Committee.

POWERS: So not a cent for any of the prisoners?

LAWYER: I'm afraid not. But if anyone deserves any kind of compensation, it would be you. I'm sorry that we are not going to be able to do anything.

Things could be worse. It takes a lot of strength and perseverance to reach for distant places, and I do not know if I have that kind of strength and perseverance. It could be too, that some of it maybe a lot of it will have to be left for others to pursue. It could be that it is better for me to remain silent at this time and see where things go. There are people who will come forward to join together for similar goals, and they will become my voice and, perhaps, my actions. If there is a way in, there must be a way out, and it is most likely the reverse of the way in.

One thing is for sure: I will never accept that it is a good thing for some human beings to keep other human beings in cages. This widespread activity is not made right by its historical uses or by legal justifications. Purposeless confinement must be rejected in its entirety. The old concepts of crime and punishment must be replaced with more rational and prosocial concepts. When the effects of imprisonment are found to be injurious to people, they must be abandoned. Prisoners should consider themselves to be expendable commodities that are being traded in commerce. They should protest when their conditions of confinement are overbearing or harmful. But most of all, prisoners should use their time to find themselves and to begin to unfold their higher selves from the inside out.

It is raining and I am standing under a tree. The wind whips the rain and drives it like a mist. I feel it on my face. Right now it is a drizzle, but the sky looks dark and gloomy. It looks like there could be a downpour at any moment. I really have no choice but to chance it, for I am going to get drenched either way. I put my head down and begin a long walk home in the rain. and now the sky does open up and come alive. Iit is thundering and flashing, and the rain is coming down in buckets. I turn to go back to the relative safety of the tree when it is struck by a bolt of lightning. A big branch comes crashing down and it looks like smoke coming off of it. I take it as a sign and walk down the center of the road in squishy sneakers, and I do not look back.

The Future is Now

THERE are a lot of strange things that go on with human beings. There are a lot of strange things that have happened with me. For example, a small bird perched on the window sill outside and preened its wings. Where did this event take place? The most obvious answer is that it took place on the window sill, right? But it all took place within my mind. My physical senses picked up a variety of signals and assembled them into the picture of the bird in my mind's eye. In other words, everything that I always thought was taking place in the external world is actually taking place in the internal world of my brain. It is a complex act that affects my perception, and it is astounding!

I try to face up to reality as much as I can. It would be much easier to drift off into some semipsychotic state or to become delusional or to be in denial. There are methods the mind uses to avoid harsh truths. The clock is always ticking, but time is never running out. Sometimes I feel that I am thousands of years old and have lived many lifetimes. There should be a solution if there is one, but nobody wants it. The hell of it is, those who need it the most do not want it. Something keeps pushing it forward while most of us are busy sitting on our assess and chewing bubble gum. Those who should be all about putting the work in want to leave it to others, but those others do not exist. It seems that there are intelligent people who do engage, but then they disengage for some reason.

The Forefathers of this nation understood full and well what would happen if the fundamental principles of liberty were lost, and this is why they insisted on a written constitution. The excessive power of government, the excessive control of government, and the excessive use of punishment by government were strictly forbidden. But these bedrock premises have been eroded since those times, and no one can put the genie back into the bottle. There are many citizens who are disgruntled, and they have good reason to be. There are too many mixed messages, too many abuses of power, and too many errors being made. Those who hold the positions of public trust have lost their way.

The way that government works is to control the behavior of those who are within its jurisdiction. The way this is done is through the creation of law. Government is nothing more than a labyrinth of law, and this law needs to be implemented, interpreted, and enforced. The way that law enforcement occurs is of ultimate value in determining the statue of liberty under a democratic republic. When the punishment is too heavy handed, the law too severe, the confinement abusive, there is a significant problem. People sense this, and there is a trend of unrest, exposure and protest that will grow exponentially.

The bus is pulling away from the prison. powers is seated up front and is chained tightly, hands, belly and ankles. He looks at the water tower and the guard towers and the building. This will be the last time he sees the ADX for a long time. He is opened to feeling something, but as the bus pulls farther and farther away, he realizes there is nothing left to feel. The bus downshifts as it makes its way around the curves and slows to make the turn onto the highway.

The drawback of falling into the trap called the criminal justice system is that once you are in it, it is nearly impossible to get out of it. It is a go-to-hell business that is nasty to its core. It may be that the best way to prevent crime is to prevent excessive punishment. Everyone cannot be locked up for everything. Future generations will look back and shake their heads in a gesture of unbelief. One of the most insidious aspects of captivity is to be blamed for having objections to it. The use of cages only breeds the use of more and more cages.

There is no question that there are people who are too dangerous to live in society, but the majority of prisoners in the federal system are not those types of people. There are better ways to achieve the goals of law and order, yet it seems they are being purposefully ignored. It is true that we human beings are indeed creatures of habit. It is very hard for us to look at things in a new light or to change up when it requires a little more work. New ideas and methods need to be developed, explored, and put into use. There are good people who can take turns pushing for the necessary reforms.

What human beings do to one another at times is something that evades logic and reason. There is an animal in all of us that can be vicious and cruel. Is there a way to train this animal, to subjugate its intent? Will human beings ever be able to get their acts together? We have this great big apparatus called civilization, but what benefit is realized when we are stuck with this ugly little lower self? If there is no way to become better human beings, then we may as well abandon any pretense that is left and give ourselves over to being the animals we are.

It could be that there is nothing more for me to say at this time. There are possibilities, but they appear more and more distant as I think about them. I hesitate to add the final lines, but I know I must. Somehow I cannot get away from this feeling of hope that I have for the entire human race. On the other hand, I can only do what I can do within my own little domain. If I happen to make it through this continuing ordeal, perhaps you will hear more from me.

Epilogue

Our litigation did improve the way the Federal Bureau of Prisons provides treatment to mentally ill prisoners. In the end, there was a settlement that I objected to because it did not provide for a compensation fund and because it did not, in my view, go far enough to ensure continuity. I have been around this system long enough to know that everything can revert to the way it was before the ADX lawsuit. Nevertheless, our efforts did blaze a trail for others to follow. It raised public awareness of the issue, it set a precedent of sorts, and it resulted in a number of tangible improvements overall.

The struggles against governmental abuse of power will continue, and criminal justice system reform will be a hot button issue for a long time to come. I hope to continue to be some part of what I now see as a widespread movement in that direction. Since leaving the ADX Supermax, I have been a participant in the programs that were established in response to the lawsuit. These are residential units that provide comprehensive treatment based on a personal growth and development format. It is exactly the way I envisioned it, and I could not ask for more. There are people here who are alive and well today even thriving in some instances because of what happened at the ADX.

As for me, I am waiting to be released within a relatively short time. My own state of mind is much better now. I continue to use THE MANUAL Program on a daily basis, and I have revised it no less than a dozen times already. There are still demons that haunt my mind by bringing back the images and feelings of dark days now in the past. But overall, I am all right with myself and my life. I still spend my days reading, writing, studying, exercising, and doing yoga. One thing that will never change with me is the absolute conviction that many lives are being destroyed by excessive imprisonment.

Made in the USA
Las Vegas, NV
27 July 2022

52186642R00075